Beyond
THE VISIBLE
EDGE

"Whoever survives a test, whatever it may be, must tell the story." That is their duty"—Elie Wiesel

"Betsy Kelleher fulfills that duty in her unique way of storytelling—exploring and conveying an excruciatingly painful life passage in down-to-earth language and metaphorical experience. The emotional depth of her words and insights will touch the very essence of feelings by those who have dealt with the devastating loss of a child. More importantly, she shows us the power of faith and belief in God's promise of eternal life, enabling us to summon the courage to take that step forward, trusting that indeed we will meet our child again in heaven."

—Ann Beatty, PhD

❧

"Taking a faith journey with the author is at once both inspiring and challenging. And throughout, most definitely interesting. As one who has experienced some of the same things in life, I highly recommend this book. At some point in life, we all go through some of the challenges she deals with. I feel her life can be an inspiration; I know it inspires me."

—Eileen Tidwell, author of the award-winning *Life in Spite of a Death Sentence, Girl on Horseback, The Goose Who Thought He Was a Chicken, When Harriet met Harlow, The Diary of Oreo Van Tyke,* and other books and articles.

❧

"Ever since childhood, Betsy has been rooted in her love of the land, her dogs and horses, and her Christian faith. In this story of her working through her grieving after the death of one of her adult sons, she realizes that although we don't always have the ability to change a situation, we most certainly can change ourselves if we simply trust in His guidance, care, and love."

—Mitzi Landsman Boyd

❧

"Jehovah Jireh, God will provide. Grief is a thief, a blessing, an opportunity, and a journey. Betsy Kelleher's transparent and beautiful memoir is a testament to God's provision and unfailing love. A sensitive and artful pilgrimage from grief to glory."

—Lynn Baber, best-selling Christian author

❧

"This book is such a great read! It tugged at every emotion! Betsy found inspiration and love in the smallest things. She has helped me to start trying to be more aware of everything. I am now looking for signs of comfort and wisdom in my life. I will definitely read this book over and over when I feel that I need extra help in my life. Betsy's words have encouraged me to look everywhere for acceptance, love and warmth."

—Toni Sbabo

❧

"Reading about Betsy Kelleher's personal experiences and knowing there is truly light at the end of the tunnel has given me some relief. I did not realize how much pain I was going through. I felt that no one else had the same feelings that she shared. Thank you, Betsy!"

—Angela Perry

✺

"A beautiful story of a woman's journey through nature—out of grief and pain into faith and acceptance."

—Lydia Friz, student in environmental science

✺

"This book contains one of the most hopeful descriptions of death I have ever read."

—B. Lynn Goodwin, Author of *Never Too Late: From Wannabe to Wife at 62*, *Talent*, and *You Want Me to Do WHAT? Journaling for Caregivers*.

✺

Beyond
THE VISIBLE
EDGE

A Grieving Mother's Pilgrimage
While Walking the Dog

Betsy Kelleher

WESTBOW
PRESS°
A DIVISION OF THOMAS NELSON
& ZONDERVAN

All Scripture quotations, unless otherwise indicated, are taken from the Holy Bible, New International Version®, NIV®. Copyright ©1973, 1978, 1984, 2011 by Biblica, Inc.™ Used by permission of Zondervan. All rights reserved worldwide. www.zondervan.com The "NIV" and "New International Version" are trademarks registered in the United States Patent and Trademark Office by Biblica, Inc.™

The New Testament in Modern English by J.B. Phillips copyright © 1960, 1972 J. B. Phillips. Administered by The Archbishops' Council of the Church of England. Used by Permission.

Scripture taken from the King James Version of the Bible.

WestBow Press books may be ordered through booksellers or by contacting:

WestBow Press
A Division of Thomas Nelson & Zondervan
1663 Liberty Drive
Bloomington, IN 47403
www.westbowpress.com
844-714-3454

All photos by Betsy Kelleher except her author photo by Russ Kelleher.
Cover photo: Beyond the visible edge of this grassy area is the secluded wetlands field.

ISBN: 978-1-9736-2210-9 (sc)
ISBN: 978-1-9736-2211-6 (hc)
ISBN: 978-1-9736-2209-3 (e)

Library of Congress Control Number: 2018903436

Print information available on the last page.

WestBow Press rev. date: 4/19/2018

A pilgrimage is usually an actual journey
to a place of spiritual significance...
but it can also be a metaphorical journey while
struggling to comprehend one's beliefs.

The pilgrimage in this memoir is both.

Remembering a son

Bob

3-29-1963 to 2-24-2013

Until we meet again in Heaven!

Contents

Acknowledgements

My earliest mentor for this memoir was B. Lynn Goodwin, a very patient and understanding instructor who offers independent study courses sponsored by Story Circle Network. She helped me shape my thoughts and words into better form as I worked through her insightful suggestions. Thank you, Lynn! I couldn't have made it this far without you.

Thanks to Peg Stomierowski Gould, who became known to me through the online Author Learning Center. She read my manuscript and offered many suggestions and comments plus a wealth of title possibilities! Peg, I greatly appreciate your feedback and encouragement.

Thanks also to Jean Erler, a member of my online writing circle with Story Circle Network, for her very astute comments and her very thorough work proofreading all my words.

While walking the Arlington Wetlands area, I met Carol Frerker, the woman who was overseeing the wetlands project. She read my manuscript, and her comments are included as a foreword. Thanks, Carol, for your work with the field as well as your encouragement for my memoir!

Finally, I am very thankful to my husband Russ for his support in so many ways, and for his willingness to allow me to spend so much time at the computer while working on this memoir. I am also thankful to my sons and their families for their love and acceptance.

I pray we never forget all that God did for our family as we experienced our loss. I thank God for what He did in my own life, and I am especially grateful for His presence as I walked in the nearby field I call my "healing place."

Foreword

As a scientist it is easy for me to understand how the significance and balance of all living things are interwoven for a healthy ecosystem. I help oversee and care for the Arlington Wetlands (which is Betsy Kelleher's backyard, so to speak).

After reading Betsy's memoir, I personally have been reminded how that balance and every living thing holds a value, not only as part of a healthy ecosystem but a healthy connection to one's true essence. After reading her book, I have been reminded to take a step back, enjoy the moment, taking in the big picture while noticing and enjoying the smaller pictures. I try to take more time to watch a butterfly float above the prairie grass or a spider strategically spin an intricate web.

This is truly a book of comfort, a reminder of life's delicate balance, and a captivating memoir how nature is the strongest thread in life's healing and simplest pleasures.

Carol Frerker

Museum Supervisor of Willoughby Heritage Farm and Arlington Wetlands
Collinsville Area Recreational District (CARD)
Willoughby Farm's Mission Statement: Preservation and education of our Midwest farm heritage and natural resources
www.collinsvillerec.com

Introduction by the Author

When I read a magazine article by a mother who had lost her young son in the Sandy Hook shootings, I burst out sobbing. Her pain touched my own heart's feelings deeply; my loss was still a fresh wound.

Whether by sudden tragedy or a drawn-out waiting, losing a child of any age is a terrible injury to a mother's heart and soul. But other losses are just as painful: wife or husband, parent or sibling, relative or friend, a pet or lifestyle.

If you are going through a journey of grief, I pray that you will find comfort and inspiration from my story. God led me on a special pilgrimage; He helps each one of us in different ways.

Grief is a normal process of healing in spite of its painful upheaval. Give it time to accomplish its restoration as you move through its stages of denial, bargaining, anger, depression, and acceptance—but remember that those stages aren't clearly marked, and they don't appear in any specific order. Talk to a counselor or minister who understands. Do something that has given you joy in the past; find a goal to work toward—something worthwhile to give you purpose. Pray for guidance. Seek comfort and insight from Scripture.

Do not turn away from your Heavenly Father because of your sadness or anger; but instead take time to be still in His loving presence. God's grace is not only the light at the end of the tunnel; it is what helps you through the darkness. Just keep going day after day; put one foot in front of the other even if those steps are tiny, and it's hard to see because of the tears. God is the Great Healer. Time spent in His presence can fill you with His love and peace and give you hope, joy, and strength. Have faith that you will reach your own healing place.

Prologue

A "HOLY LAND" OF WEEDS

*L*ooking eastward from our front porch toward the edge of our mobile home community, I see a grassy area where children play and residents walk their dogs. Just beyond that grassy area is a hidden field where I walked a dog while grieving the loss of a grown son.

The field was not always hidden from view; when I first saw it, it was an open piece of cropland adjoining the grassy area. One tall mulberry tree and some brush marked the property line. I respected the field's boundaries—although I picked a few stems of wheat once for a fall table arrangement. And then the mulberry tree was cut down, and an earthen berm—like a protective levy—was built along the back of the grassy area. That berm became the visible edge of our mobile home community.

Beyond that berm, the hidden field is now part of the Arlington Wetlands, a reclaimed natural conservation project for educational and recreational use. It's a small acreage of grasses, weeds, and flowers with a mowed pathway winding around the center of it past a pond, a bench, birdhouses on metal posts, and signs to educate hikers. Surrounded by trees on three sides and the berm in front, it is a secluded place of nature's solitude. I call it my healing place.

THE SECLUDED WETLANDS FIELD

I never would have found that field except for a newly acquired Boston terrier named Ribbons who had been trained to poop only in her own back yard. We wouldn't have had Ribbons except that we wanted a replacement after our first dog, Lil, died unexpectedly. One thing so often leads to another, and only in retrospection can we see God's hand in it all.

The minute she saw my husband, Motif's Diamond Lil seemed to know she was meant to be our dog. A playfully demanding, very loving little Boston terrier, she entered our lives the year after my grown son was diagnosed with cancer. For three years, she made me smile when I didn't feel like smiling—until her sudden death one evening, three months after I'd lost my son.

God had helped me through those three months, and I thought I was doing better than most grieving mothers—until Lil was gone.

Suddenly, my losses were overwhelming. After a time, I wondered if another dog might be a small comfort. But on an August morning in 2013, I found myself dealing with a newly acquired Boston named "Ribbons" that did not relieve herself for three days—except once on the carpet. Walking that unsettled dog evolved into an unusual journey of spiritual renewal that I now call my pilgrimage.

My husband and I live in a mobile home park of 200 homes. Some of them, like ours, have a back yard that drops off into Edelhardt Lake. Other homes line the roads that loop around on each side of the lake. The grassy area at the edge of our community is near one of those side roads. That was where I took our problem pooch, hoping she would do her business somewhere besides on the carpet!

Fortunately, there in that grassy area one morning, she figured it out. And there at the edge of that grassy area, I noticed a new pathway into the adjoining property—the former cropland now hidden from view by the man-made earthen berm. For years I had wondered what that berm was hiding, and this new opening was an invitation I couldn't resist. I didn't know it then, but I had discovered the entrance to my own private "Holy Land."

It was six months since Bob had passed away after his struggle against cancer. I had prayed for a miracle that never came, and too many questions and doubts were eating away at my Christian convictions. Perhaps a pilgrimage was exactly what I needed. God apparently had worked out the details, and I didn't have to travel to some distant shrine; this place was within walking distance.

The rising sun colors the sky over that field and sometimes touches every cloud with a rosy blush before fading into early daylight. Those impressive sunrise mornings had pointed me in that direction long before I knew what waited for me beyond the mobile home park's grassy area.

As I learned the story behind the field, I was fascinated by an intriguing coincidence. The thirty-acre farm property had been sold in 2008 to become part of a natural wetlands restoration project—the same year that my son was diagnosed with terminal cancer. What significance—if any—connected the beginning of Bob's cancer journey with the plan for this nearby field's restoration?

While the field was cropland, it had no fence; and I could have walked through it at any time. I entered that area only when it became open to the public for recreational and educational purposes in 2013—the same year Bob died. Because of the corresponding dates, I was strangely drawn to this nearby field. The year 2008 marked the beginning of serious change for Bob's life and for the farm property—while the year 2013 marked a reawakening to new dimensions.

I truly believe that our new dog was God's instrument to help me discover the path into that field. I'm sure now that every detail was on God's omniscient calendar, and none of it was a coincidence. I believe God knew how much that place would mean to me at this precise moment in time.

I re-entered the field soon after my initial discovery. As I followed the mowed pathway into the secluded acreage surrounded by trees, I saw only weeds and grasses and a few yellow flowers in bloom. But as I continued to walk the dog in that nearby field, I became enthralled by the holy mystique of this place.

I didn't hear a voice from Heaven or see a vision, but I soon understood that God had led me into that field to help me deal with my grief. Where soybeans or winter wheat once grew, I reaped a very different harvest. My saddened heart found comfort in the cheerful influence of bright flowers and lovely grasses surrounding a peaceful pond. I sat on a bench by that pond and cried tears of sadness—and the joyful songs of birds lifted my spirits. Within that secluded field surrounded by tall trees under a sheltering canopy of sky and cloud, I felt enclosed by God's healing presence.

There in that field, God showed me nature's testimony of His Sovereign glory. As He worked in my heart to restore my faith, I gradually found a new perspective on life and death.

Part One

WAITING FOR A MIRACLE

Chapter One

COVERED BY GRACE

*B*ob was the middle child of three from my first marriage—between Mark, my firstborn, and David, my youngest. I had struggled in that marriage for forty-two years, telling myself I was a good Christian for staying even though I was miserable. Bob was forty the year Wes and I agreed on a divorce. All three boys had families of their own by then. They were more disappointed than surprised.

I remarried. I had met Russ at the barn where I boarded my horses, and we had ridden together in the pasture behind the stable. We were both retired by the time we married, and life was good. Russ and I had a wonderful relationship, even though I still felt guilty for leaving my first husband.

Horses had been my lifelong passion. After years of effort, I was enjoying moderate success as an equestrian writer. I was the author of two published books, and I wrote a monthly newspaper column in the *Illinois Horse Network* newspaper. Under the heading "Sometimes God Uses Horses," each column shared a horse-related experience with a Christian application. I was just finishing my December column that Monday morning, November 17, 2008, when the call came.

"Hi Mom, it's your son Bob." I smiled at how he always began his phone calls, as if I wouldn't immediately recognize his voice. "I'm not doing so good. I'm in the hospital." My smile disappeared as he talked about high blood calcium, anemia, failing kidneys, and bone lesions. I felt my chest tighten; I held my breath. It sounded serious, even before he told me he was in the ICU. I had questions, but he sounded weak.

"Let me talk to Kim." I knew his wife would have answers. She soon pronounced that word that I dreaded. *Cancer.* Feeling sick, Bob had gone to the emergency room on Sunday. Tests showed an advanced stage of multiple myeloma.

This was a cancer I'd never heard of, so I looked it up in my big Mayo Clinic health book. And then I sat staring into space for a moment while trying to process what I'd read. Multiple myeloma is a cancer of the bone marrow; it's a blood cancer that eats away at the bones. It is treatable to the point of producing temporary remission, but there is no cure. It is a terminal illness.

What? How did that happen?

Bob had mentioned back pain several times that summer when we talked. His doctor prescribed physical therapy, but then his pain got worse. No one had suspected that cancer was causing the pain, not even his doctor.

My personal prayers didn't seem enough for something this big, so I sent emails to everyone I knew. Experience had taught me that the prayers of many could have miraculous results. God had answered prayer in the past, and I believed He would do it again.

Twenty years earlier, my youngest son David, then twenty-three years old, had almost died of liver failure from hepatitis. For three weeks, I stayed with him in the hospital, going home only to clean up and change clothes. David's father had kept busy at work, visiting only twice. He didn't know what to do for David or how to give me the support I needed. I was the one who talked to the doctors. I was the one who signed papers to approve the transplant. I felt terribly alone and anxious while waiting for the outcome. I watched my son slip in and out of a coma for five days, and then I was told one morning that he had twenty-four hours to live.

Frequent phone calls from a friend with medical experience helped me cope. Pam had been my best friend for ten years since supervising the training of my first horse—the experience shared in my first book. Her advice may have saved David's life; because of her, I knew to turn him on his side to prevent choking when he became nauseous. She also suggested I could help the nurses by checking the flow from the IV bags. Whether it really did any good or not, doing something positive was better than sitting and worrying.

God took care of us during those stressful weeks, and I truly believe He let me see His hand at work in all the details. I sensed the support of prayers for David, and I witnessed the miracle of a successful liver transplant. I was deeply grateful for the liver that came just in time, even though I knew it was donated by a grieving family who lost their own loved one. I thanked God for the eventual success of the transplant in spite of a few early episodes of rejection.

God's loving presence was with me through it all. I sensed His power and control. In spite of the fear and worry, this whole situation was an experience that strengthened my faith.

David's miraculous transplant confirmed my belief that God could heal, but I already believed. I had experienced a physical healing myself ten years earlier. With two healings in our family and everyone now praying for Bob, I had great hopes for another miracle.

In early December a few weeks after Bob's call from the hospital, I went to bed saying fervent prayers for Bob's healing. I remember waking up the next morning with a song of praise flowing through me. Music had always been a strong influence in my life, but I hadn't sung or heard this particular song for many years. Yet now here it was suddenly filling me with the joy of God's protective power: "He's my rock, He's my fortress, He's my deliverer, in Him will I trust! Praise the name of Jesus!" Similar words are found in Psalm 18:2, in Psalm 114:2, and in 2 Samuel 22:2.

I emailed a friend to share my experience. She emailed back that

God sometimes gives us a song or a special message of encouragement called a grace covering. "You are not alone in this. God is present and doing many things to strengthen you."

When I told Bob about the song, he wanted to hear it—so I found it for him on YouTube. I believed this grace covering was more than just encouragement; it gave me the assurance that God was with us. I believed He was preparing a miracle.

Perhaps that song was more for me than for Bob. Looking back, I believe God meant it to guide me through all of life's trials. The words reminded me to depend on God for my strength and hope. I remembered my friend's words: "You are not alone."

When did I stop singing that song? Why did I stop?

Chapter Two

ROAD TO REMISSION

For four years and three months, I waited for the miracle that would heal my son. I truly believed God could heal, even at the last minute; and I believed He could use doctors or any other means. Was I wrong to expect a miracle? Shouldn't we always believe in miracles?

The doctors could not treat the cancer until Bob's failing kidneys were functioning. He needed dialysis three times a week at first. Finally in March his kidneys were working, and dialysis was no longer necessary.

Meanwhile, because he had five compression fractures in his spine, Bob was scheduled in January for a procedure called a vertebroplasty. This was an operation to inject special cement into the fractures to stabilize his spine so he could walk. The doctors did a series of procedures, working on different sections each time. During one procedure, however, Bob had a cardiac arrest. They brought him back, but his spine had been damaged. He was now six inches shorter and looked somewhat like the Hunchback of Notre Dame. He was transferred to a rehab center from the end of January until the middle of March. Kim stayed at his side.

Although it was a miracle that Bob was still alive, I had to hold back tears of despair when I saw him so bent over—so deformed. I was never again able to hug him with the same affectionate energy as I had before his spine was damaged. He looked too fragile. The cancer had already taken a part of him from me.

I was grateful for the Facebook page Kim and Bob created to keep friends and family updated. I followed Bob's cancer journey by their posts, which probably saved them a lot of time not having to answer my inquiring phone calls.

They say denial is the first stage of the grief process. I couldn't deny that Bob had cancer, but I could refuse to accept that it was terminal. I was determined to fix this—to find a cure to change Bob's prognosis. Did I believe I could do more than his doctors? I was his mother; I had to do *something*!

In a discussion group one day, I heard someone say, "When we feel helpless and we don't know what to do, we just do something we *can* do." I realized I was doing exactly that—spending hours on the internet researching cancer. It became an obsession.

Finally I understood why my first husband had spent so much time in his office back in 1988 instead of being with our youngest son in the hospital. After his first visit—seeing David's condition before the liver transplant—he knew he couldn't fix it, and he couldn't face what might happen. Work was his escape.

My escape from Bob's situation was searching for a solution. The internet was full of stories of amazing healings through alternative methods. I wanted to believe those stories. Perhaps such hope was too naive, but it kept me going.

I learned that specific tests can determine the type of cancer present, and different types of cancer need different treatments. Not all doctors do those tests. Choosing one's doctor is a critical part of any health care, whether for cancer or any other health issue. I believe we must be our own advocate—to search for knowledge, to ask questions that lead to wise decisions, and to be responsible for our God-given bodies as much as possible.

When Bob entered the hospital where his diagnosis was made, he trusted the doctors that worked with him because they were highly recommended. Bob believed that God had put him where he was for a reason, and he didn't have a lot of time to figure it out. I hoped my research could give him more information to help him understand his treatments.

Spending time on the internet, I learned about foods and pills that worked to fight cancer. I subscribed to newsletters, and I purchased books. The internet helped spread the word that I was looking, and I received countless emails and mailings from doctors and publishing companies selling books about alternative treatments. Bob bought a few of the books I mentioned to him, and we discussed his options.

For a whole year, Bob endured regular chemo and radiation treatments. Blood tests showed his cancer markers were going down. The goal of remission still had not been reached, so the doctors scheduled a stem cell transplant. Information I found online said that such a transplant was a risky procedure of last resort. Bob's doctor assured him that it could add one or two years to his remission, making it three or four years instead of the usual two. I was thankful for all that his doctors did, but I wanted more than remission; I wanted actual healing.

The doctors planned for Bob to spend most of July in the hospital. On June 24, he had a procedure to insert a catheter before five days of injections to help his bones create more stem cells. As an outpatient at Loyola University Center for Health, he was hooked up to a machine for six hours while ten million of his stem cells were collected in one day. In early July, he entered the hospital for strong chemo—the worst part—to kill off all his bone marrow. After three weeks of isolation and after the saved stem cells were reintroduced, Kim posted on Facebook that he would have to come home to a "low-bacteria" environment for two more weeks of isolation.

Her next update said: "…Bob has come home to a clean house! He's still nauseous and his throat and mouth hurt, but he's glad to be home. A lot of you have asked when Bob will be normal again (which is an excellent opportunity for humor but I'll resist the temptation). It will take half a year for his blood counts to be considered normal." Kim's sense of humor always made me smile in spite of Bob's dismal circumstances.

A post in mid-August brought another smile: "In general, Bob is miserable, and he feels gross from the chemo and stem cell transplant. I have to admit he looks quite pitiful, but so cute. A little like a droopy-eyed hound dog if you can imagine that (and this description brought a smile to his face). We take walks, he's on the treadmill daily, and he has finished three photo albums."

For a year, I kept track of Bob's struggle while going about my own life. Russ and I had been married for six years, and he understood what I was going through; he had lost a son of his own. We owned four horses then, and we often went riding in a nearby wooded park. Our rides through the peaceful beauty of nature helped me to relax. But no mother can forget her son; I was constantly praying for Bob's healing.

On October 12, 2009, Bob posted an update that answered my most important question. "There's a lot to be thankful for. My cancer is pretty much in full remission, and I am regaining my strength and returning to work soon." I had heard rumors of remission, but this made it official. Now I could finally do my happy dance.

Chapter Three

HOME FOR CHRISTMAS

When my youngest son David invited us to his home in Pennsylvania for Christmas in 2009, I was overjoyed. Our whole family would be together to celebrate Bob's remission! I was looking forward to this holiday with all my boys, and I was grateful that Russ was willing to make the long drive from Illinois and back.

That last morning on the road, we left the motel and stopped for breakfast at Cracker Barrel. I was in the ladies' room feeling anxious about the weather (we had seen a few snowflakes) and about finding David's house. Then I heard someone singing, and the words were loud and clear: "Follow Me, I'll lead you home." Even though it was Amy Grant's voice on Cracker Barrel's PA system, I believed God had directed those words to me to help me trust that everything would work out.

This Christmas with my family meant much more to me than the usual holiday get-together. After the divorce, the boys had spent holidays with their dad because he was alone. One year all three boys and their families spent a whole week with him. They had invited us to join them, but Russ said he wasn't going to spend a whole week with my ex-husband. It might have spoiled Christmas for all of us. I didn't see any of them, and I cried a lot that Christmastime because I felt so left out. Why hadn't I thought to talk to them about how to handle this change in our family situation? I shouldn't have assumed they would understand.

During phone conversations with each of my sons, I finally shared my feelings; and they adjusted their Thanksgiving plans. Russ and I drove to Bob's home in Chicago in 2006 to spend two days with everyone, and then we left before my ex-husband arrived. I was surprised to discover that time with my sons and their families was more wonderful than ever before! Being happy in my marriage with Russ, I no longer had what may have been an unhealthy need for their attention. I was free to simply enjoy their company.

When Russ and I went out to the car to leave at the end of our visit, Mark walked out with us, then Bob came out, and then David. I was amused that they followed their birth order. I cried as we drove away—not only from the usual sadness of leaving family—but because my sons' farewell gesture meant so much to me. As all three sons waved goodbye from Bob's front porch, I saw a picture of acceptance, belonging, and love. That precious image is still burned into my memory.

It was now three years later, Christmas of 2009, and Russ and I were spending a whole week with my three sons and their families in David's home in Pennsylvania. We didn't have to leave early this time, since the boys' father had passed away the previous April after a stroke. I know the boys felt his loss during this first Christmas without him, and my own emotions were still in turmoil. We didn't talk about it.

The past year had been difficult for all of us. Even while dealing with his cancer, Bob had disposed of his dad's home and contents, aided by his brothers and an auction. I had helped some, but it hadn't been easy to watch former possessions and memories laid out to be auctioned off to strangers. The entire process had been indescribably painful.

With all of that now behind us, we celebrated Bob's remission. Words could not describe my joy at finally being together with my three sons and their families for a real family Christmas. I was relieved that a year of cancer treatments was over, and I didn't want to think about the future. I hugged Bob—carefully—every chance I had. I'm thankful I didn't know then that this would be our last joyful Christmas together.

David had a lovely home in a peaceful wooded setting. LuAnn was a considerate hostess, and her meals were bounteous. We probably ate too much. We played games at the spacious dining room table surrounded by windows that revealed a wooded hillside adorned with snow. We laughed at their cat, Tommy, how he sometimes watched over us from his position on a high cupboard. Russ and I usually went to bed early downstairs, giving the younger adults a chance to share their own thoughts with each other.

We took family photos around the big, elaborately decorated Christmas tree—photos of each family separately and photos of everyone together with Bob in the center. His spinal condition didn't show except that he was shorter than everyone else, and his head was bald then. We went shopping. One day we drove in three cars to Lancaster's Amish country for a sightseeing trip.

When the time came, it took all my courage to leave my family; and I dreaded the long drive back to Illinois. Gratefully, I reminded myself of those words, "Follow Me, I'll lead you home."

Chapter Four

MOTIF'S DIAMOND LIL

Christmas was over except for one more present. Our long drive home from Pennsylvania included one stop on the way to pick up a dog named "Motif's Diamond Lil." She was my Christmas present for Russ.

We had first seen Lil in August at the Illinois State Fair, about the time that Bob left the hospital after his stem cell transplant. Russ and I attended the Fair each year, and we enjoyed watching the horse shows and walking through the horse stall areas. As we passed one aisle of stalls in a building near the Coliseum, we saw a playpen where three black and white Boston terriers lay sleeping.

One dog suddenly stood up on her hind legs, pawing excitedly at the playpen railing and reaching out toward my husband. He picked her up, and she licked his face with unusual enthusiasm. Laughing, he put her down to wipe his face. Russ had grown up around an uncle's Boston terrier, and he loved the breed.

She ran for a toy, a green rubber pencil, and brought it in her mouth to him, again pawing in his direction. How cute! I wondered why one dog would get so excited while the others didn't. I also noticed the hairless scars on her back. We smiled at her antics and walked on. We didn't need a dog; we had enough to do with four horses.

I later remembered something Russ said whenever we shopped at Goodwill. I would say I didn't need anything, and he would smile and reply, "You never know until you see it!" And I would often see something that spoke to me like that dog spoke to him.

Lil's personality had made a first impression that my husband couldn't forget. He talked about that dog for months, always wishing we had the names of her owners. I listened to his frequent, unrelenting regrets until I decided that perhaps he needed that dog—so I needed to find that very dog!

Now Lil was not the same dog I later walked on the paths of my healing field, but we would never have gotten a second dog if Lil hadn't entered our lives first.

I searched the internet for Boston terrier breeders, and I emailed horse owners who might have been showing at the state fair. I finally found someone who knew about the little Boston with scars on her back. I called the dog's owner, and then I told Russ the good news. The dog we had seen at the state fair would be his Christmas present! I arranged to pick her up on our way home from our family holiday in Pennsylvania.

After our first evening with Lil's exuberant, demanding personality, we almost sent her back. Her former owners had other dogs, and they believed Lil would be happier as an only pet. We soon understood why. She insisted on being the center of attention. She wouldn't leave us alone to eat supper or watch TV. She was constantly in our faces, joyfully bestowing wet licky kisses with sudden energy. We felt bombarded.

A borrowed crate gave all of us space to adjust. Within a few days, Lil had captured our hearts. The same exuberant, demanding personality that almost got her sent back also made us love her.

Lil's antics were priceless. She would drop a toy at my feet and then scoot backward with her head held low over her extended front paws and her little rear end pointed upward. She would get my attention with a strong woof or two, while that mischievous look in her eyes challenged me to grab the toy. She usually beat me to it, but she always gave me a second chance.

LIL WANTS TO PLAY

Two rubber toys had come with her: the green pencil and a purple dumbbell. She loved to fetch, and it didn't matter which toy I tossed; she would bring it back to me again and again and again. When she got tired, she would hunker down and chew on the toy. I enjoyed playing with Lil; she was so much fun! She was the perfect distraction from my worries.

Friends who saw Lil for the first time usually asked about those hairless scars on her back. Her owners had told us she'd had a serious infection called MRSA, or Methicillin-resistant Staphylococcus Aureus. A veterinarian had saved her life, but she couldn't be bred again. I didn't really mind her scars; I wanted to believe they were part of the reason we got her—because she could no longer have puppies and because she wanted to be our only dog.

For three and a half years, Lil filled our days with fun and laughter and gave our quiet old lives more love than we imagined a dog could give. She was our precious little girl. She was supposed to be my husband's dog, but I ended up feeding her, playing with her, and walking her.

Our favorite story about Lil always brought a smile. I was sitting at my computer one day when Lil ran into my office and pawed excitedly on my leg. I got up and followed her back to the living room where Russ sat on the sofa with a guilty grin on his face. "OK, what happened?" I asked. "What did you do?"

"I was trying to read the TV guide, and she wouldn't stop pestering me. So I popped her lightly on her bottom with the rolled up paper. I knew when she ran out of here that she was going to snitch on me!" We couldn't help but love Lil's spunky personality. Lil was a special blessing.

Chapter Five

THE STRUGGLE RESUMES!

Kim had told us Bob might have ten years. I didn't say anything. I hoped for more, but I feared he might have less. My online research indicated that this type of cancer often returns in two years after a patient has gone into remission.

Bob's doctor had done the stem cell transplant because he believed it could extend the remission to three or four years. Unfortunately, he was wrong. After two years of remission, even with the stem cell transplant, Bob's cancer returned the fall of 2011. I couldn't believe two years had gone by so fast. I wondered how many were left. This whole situation seemed so unreal.

During those two years, Bob had worked remotely from home on his computer with minimal trips to his office. It was the perfect arrangement for him, since he could drive only by boosting himself up with pillows because of his shortness and spinal curvature. Since the cancer was back, Bob knew he would be involved with more cancer treatments. He took temporary sick leave.

While Bob's doctors were working toward his second remission, I found myself dealing with the loss of my favorite horse. Traveller had been my safest riding partner for fourteen years; he was more reliable, more sensible, and more caring than any horse I'd ever owned. Six years earlier he had been diagnosed with EPM, or equine protozoal myeloencephalitis; his system had been invaded by a parasite.

Fortunately, our minister's wife happened to have a free sample of a new product that could treat EPM. I saw it as a gift from God, since the only FDA-approved drug was so expensive. Although I had two other horses—Lady, my Tennessee Walking Horse, and a Spotted Saddle Horse named Rocky—I preferred Traveller's calm, confident nature. And because the free product worked, I was able to enjoy riding him for five more years.

As he got older, however, he became weaker. For the past year he had been unsafe to ride, so I took care of him the best I could—until the day I saw how unsteady he was as I led him from his stall. I had known this day would come, but it was hard to accept it was already here. As much as I loved this horse, I knew I couldn't hold onto him any longer.

On January 9, 2012, the vet on call took care of it all with compassion. Friends came to support me. In spite of my emotional pain, God helped me through those last hours. As I thanked Traveller one last time for all he meant to me, I saw this experience as a foretaste of the future. I thought of Bob, struggling for his life.

There's even a name for such a time—when you see a future loss coming and you have to watch helplessly until it takes its victim. It's called "anticipatory" grief, but I don't like that name; I think "apprehensive" is more fitting. "Anticipation" applies to welcome events in my opinion, such as Christmas and birthdays—not death.

Later that month, Bob's blood tests showed the cancer markers coming down, almost to the point of remission again. It was good news, even though Bob's doctor had told him the cancer might come back sooner after a second remission. I was keeping track and still praying for that miracle. But Bob's next call came from the hospital.

A Facebook update had mentioned that Bob was taking an antibiotic because of a fever and breathing problems. At first they thought he had pneumonia, but then they decided it was a bronchial infection. In mid-January, they discovered he had something called C-diff, short for Clostridium difficile. A very serious infection, it gave him diarrhea and painful cramps. Doctors prescribed more antibiotics.

I thought of the hairless scars on Lil's back from the MRSA infection, and I knew MRSA and C-diff were both highly dangerous. Would the doctors be able to overcome Bob's infection as successfully as Lil's vet had solved hers?

By the end of February, Bob was in the hospital again because the C-diff had returned. More antibiotics—but still not enough. The C-diff came back a third time. Cancer treatments had been postponed during each round of antibiotics, and they were again postponed during thirty days of an even stronger antibiotic. And then finally, the C-diff was gone—leaving Bob with severe neuropathy pain.

During those times when the doctors had to postpone Bob's chemotherapy, I urged him to try a natural alternative. He tried a few different treatments, but one mixture had a sickening taste and another didn't seem to work. Natural treatments are slower than the more toxic traditional drugs, and Bob's doctors favored chemo. They put him back on traditional treatments as soon as possible.

Chapter Six

PRECIOUS DAYS

On March 22, 2012, I took the Amtrak to spend two days with Bob and his family. I worried how I would find him outside the busy downtown Chicago station, but I should have known that God's timing is always perfect. As I walked out the door, Bob was driving by and watching for me, ready to pull over.

He drove me around downtown Chicago for an hour before going home. He pointed out the building where he had worked, and he drove along the waterfront past flowering trees on that gorgeous spring day. He drove past Millennium Park, and I was fascinated by the Cloud Gate, also called "The Bean," a sculpture of polished stainless steel thirty feet high and sixty-six feet long. As he drove, I took many photos. Whenever I look at them, I am grateful for that precious hour that we had together.

Kim was working that day, so Bob and I made a big batch of homemade potato soup for lunch. After seeing an afternoon movie, we returned home to spend time with Kim and their three girls still living at home. Alison would soon be twenty-three years old, and the twins, Hannah and Sharon, would be twenty-two.

On Friday, we celebrated Bob's forty-ninth birthday at our

favorite Benihana restaurant. Back at Bob's home, we enjoyed listening to their girls playing piano and violin and singing. I thanked God for all the ways He had blessed this family. These lovely girls had often sung in church, and I was proud of their abilities. One cherished memory was a family Thanksgiving meal when they sang the doxology in beautiful harmony in place of a spoken blessing.

Two days go by so quickly, I thought to myself as Bob dropped me off at the train station later that evening. Every moment had been so precious. How many more would I have with him?

Could I be as calm as Bob seemed to be—if I was the one fighting cancer? I was proud of his faith. I never heard him complain or ask, "Why me?" I seriously wanted to know how he was feeling about all of this, but I couldn't bring myself to ask. I knew he was going through the treatments just to be with his family as long as possible. He was constantly working with Kim, helping her get ready for what lay ahead, and we had talked about his financial plans during my visit. He was setting up trust funds for Kim and the girls. It sounded like a practical solution, but so finalistic.

A friend had warned me that I might try to bargain with God. At the time, I didn't think that was a good idea. But now I was getting desperate. I knew God could heal, and I reminded Him that He'd touched both David and me. Why wasn't Bob being healed too? His family needed him! Was that a form of bargaining? Whatever it was, it didn't bring the desired miracle.

Back in January, Bob had announced a surprise. Despite his ongoing cancer treatments, he arranged a family vacation for all of us in June. At a neighborhood yard sale, he had won a one-week stay at a Florida time-share resort! The three brothers would share a lovely three-bedroom condo apartment within the resort, while Russ and I stayed in a nearby motel. Bob had taken advantage of this opportunity to get us all together—perhaps to spend enjoyable time with his family while he could.

Rather than take a plane, Russ and I decided to drive. It was an exhausting adventure, but we arrived safely in spite of a flat tire.

There were lots of possible activities in the area, but not all of them were things that Russ and I wanted to do. When the rest of the family spent a whole day at a theme park or fishing, I wished we were younger with more energy. But I treasured every moment I was able to spend with them.

I thoroughly enjoyed watching my grandkids swimming and playing in the pool as we rested in lounge chairs in the sun. One evening we had a birthday party for David's wife, LuAnn. I wouldn't have missed that summer vacation with my family for anything.

Chapter Seven

MISSIONS AND BLUEBELLS

A few weeks after our Florida vacation, the whole family was surprised by Bob's announcement that he and Alison would go on a week-long mission trip to Nicaragua the end of July. He told his church about his decision to follow God's prompting when he gave an inspiring testimony that was recorded on a DVD. It is still on YouTube.

He returned from the trip feeling sick, but he said he was glad he had gone. Without that mission trip, we wouldn't have had Bob's recorded testimony that later meant so much to all of us. It's the only way I can still hear Bob's voice, even though I find it emotionally difficult.

I was so very proud of his words. He told how he had to face living a shorter life. He said that cancer taught him "to make my days count." He briefly shared how he had found his faith at a summer church camp that our family had attended. "I can trust the Lord wherever I am," he said. "My prayer is not to be healed, but to let me be useful." I prayed for his healing anyway—hoping God might still give us a miracle.

In I Peter 4:12-13, we are told to rejoice when we share in

the sufferings of Christ. I hope that Bob experienced a special blessing within his own suffering. I would often pray that He felt an awareness of God's presence. In 2 Timothy 4:7 (NIV), Paul said: "I have fought the good fight. I have finished the race. I have kept the faith." I thought of Bob whenever I read those words.

Bob and Kim came for a brief visit in November, just after Thanksgiving. Bob connected an external hard drive as backup for my old computer. I couldn't find the software disc to run it, so he actually wrote a program to back up the data. I was very glad he knew how to do that. On the first of each month, I clicked on a desktop icon, and everything was saved automatically. This simple security task became a precious ritual, and I remember often whispering, "Thanks Bob."

He was scheduled to see his doctor in Chicago the day after our visit. The news wasn't good; the chemo wasn't working anymore. On December 17, they tried an older, harsher drug which made Bob so sick that he could hardly eat or drink for three days. He decided he didn't want any more treatments. He signed up with hospice.

Little things sometimes happen that seem to have no importance until later. The day after Bob's chemo treatment, I went shopping at Goodwill. I saw a lovely porcelain cup decorated with cobalt bluebells outlined in gold, and the inside had a gold patterned edge. Printed in red on the bottom was "Made in Russia" along with other markings. It was so lovely that I wanted to buy it. When I told Russ about it later, he said I should have.

We were back in town the next day, so I decided to see if the cup was still there. It was, and I bought it. I thought it was so pretty that I texted a picture of it to Kim. She texted back, "Did you know bluebells are Bob's favorite flower?" I did not know that! The cup is now in my china cabinet in the living room. Whenever I look at it, I remember that Bob loved bluebells. I treasure this cup from Goodwill as one of God's simple blessings—worth much more to me than the three dollars I paid.

Chapter Eight

OUR CHRISTMAS MIRACLE

From the information our family had, we believed that Bob might have three months left. We decided to spend a few days together with him while he could still enjoy our company.

On the last day of December, my oldest son Mark flew in from California with his wife Susan and their two kids, Taylre and Travis. David drove from Pennsylvania with his wife LuAnn and their daughter, Megan, and they came through a snow storm that was so bad they almost turned back. I took Amtrak to a station south of Chicago where I thought David could stop on his way and pick me up. Even his GPS had problems finding that station, which turned out to be nothing more than a bench within a sheltered enclosure. David found it, however, and he was there waiting for me when I got off the train. He arranged for my room in his hotel and drove me back and forth to Bob's home. Enjoying breakfast each morning with his family was another blessing. If Mark had stayed at the same hotel, it would have been perfect—but he had points to redeem from a different place.

We all spent two days with Bob, trying not to tire him too

27

much since he had a bad chest cold and could hardly talk without coughing. So we simply surrounded him with our loving presence. On Sunday afternoon, I counted thirteen of us in his bedroom where he lay propped up on the bed with pillows. Most of us sat on chairs. A few stood. Hannah stretched out on the bed with her head against the headboard and one arm sometimes around Bob. Kim stretched out beside her. Travis sat on the foot of the bed, and Susan found room on the windowsill.

Mark and David teased the twins about their boyfriends. We sounded happy as we talked and laughed and reminisced. Family— together one last time—making the most of those precious hours.

We were blessed to have those few days, and I am very aware that not everyone has such a sad privilege. I felt God's love in that room—supporting and comforting us as we went through this difficult time. For now, we still had each other. I retreated once to the kitchen downstairs, where one of the girls and I shared a long emotional hug and a few tears.

The three girls still at home wanted to stay close to their dad for as long as possible. The twins—Sharon, a model, and Hannah, a beautician—would surely support each other as they always did. Alison's music was her joy; she gave piano and violin lessons, and she sang and played in several small groups. The oldest girl, Ambre, was married with children and lived in another state. They came to visit later.

The three at home seemed to be dealing with the situation quite well, I thought. They had been raised in church, and I assumed their belief in God would get them through this. I assumed my own faith would get me through it, and we would all be fine because God was with us.

Alison had stubbornly held onto her belief that God would heal her Papi (her endearing term for Bob). I didn't realize then that her father's death would be so devastating for her faith. Christian beliefs do not prevent our sadness, and loss sometimes cuts deeper than we realize.

We assume our children will get old like us someday. I had assumed that Bob would see all of his four daughters get married. He had already walked Ambre down the aisle; I imagined how the other three would feel on their wedding day.

On Monday, while everyone else was downstairs eating lunch, I sat alone with Bob. I read a letter to him to thank him for all the things he had ever done for me and to thank God for the son he had been to me. I had hesitated to write such an emotional letter, but I have always been glad that I did. I would have regretted not telling Bob how much he meant to me. Words from the heart bring a certain healing of their own. Kim later read the letter to him one more time.

On New Year's Day, David dropped me off at the little Amtrak station that looked like a bus stop. He waited until I boarded the train before they waved goodbye, and he drove away. My trip home was a bitter-sweet beginning for the New Year—but a small piece of good news was on the way.

During Bob's chest cold, he had held a high temperature for twenty-four hours. I knew that some cancer clinics used heat to treat cancer, and I wondered if Bob's fever could possibly be part of God's healing. Yes, I knew it was wishful thinking, but I still hoped for a miracle.

Bob soon announced the results of his latest blood test. Whether it was the harsh chemo, the fever, the prayer, or everything combined—the cancer marker had gone down from 1100 to forty-eight. Bob told me the pain in his bones was gone. We called it our Christmas miracle—this amazing lowering of the cancer marker along with the irreplaceably poignant time we'd had together as a family.

Chapter Nine

TWO WEEKS

*T*he doctor wanted Bob to have another strong chemo treatment as soon as possible, before the cancer could regain strength again. Since the last treatment had made him sick enough to sign up with hospice, Bob wasn't ready to face that experience again. I've always wondered what would have happened if Bob had agreed to that treatment.

Feeling better, he decided to sign out of hospice in early January of 2013. He wanted to try a special vegan diet that was supposed to fight cancer. His decision worried me; but it was his decision, and I understood. Unfortunately, his next blood test showed the cancer had taken over again, just as the doctor had feared it would. Bob reluctantly agreed to another treatment scheduled for Valentine's Day. I was glad; maybe one more treatment would work the miracle.

I had just snuggled into bed the evening of February 13 when Bob called. He pleasantly wished me a Happy Valentine's Day, and then he casually said his doctor had canceled the chemo treatment based on the latest blood test.

"They can't do anything more," he told me. "I've got two weeks." His voice sounded calm and unemotional. The news caught me totally off guard. It didn't make sense. *TWO WEEKS?* I think at that moment, my mind could not accept what I had just heard. It was easier to push it aside until I could deal with it later.

"You know I love you." Those were my only words. I couldn't think of anything else to say. Why couldn't I have said something comforting to support Bob at that moment? What could I have said? I felt numb as I tried to absorb the news. I couldn't even cry.

I went back to bed. I lay there awake for awhile; and then I got up and called Susan, Mark's wife, in California. Mark was talking to Bob on another phone, so I told Susan the news. I was reaching for some kind of reassurance that no one could give.

Early the next morning I sent Bob an email: "What can I do to help you most?" A few hours later, he emailed back, "I don't want you to keep looking for cures. I do appreciate all you've done over the years, and I love you very much."

Two days later, I got an email about a pill that a New York doctor was using to treat cancer. AHCC is a mushroom extract that strengthens the immune system. I was desperate at this point; I was grabbing at anything even if it didn't make sense to anyone else. Despite Bob's request, I texted Kim that I would order the pills to be sent to Bob.

Bob called me that afternoon. "Mom," he began in a voice that sounded frustrated, almost angry, "Stop it! Stop looking for cures. Let go!"

Let go? What mother wants to let go of her son? For years, I had been searching for a cure. It was the only way I could cope. I didn't know how to let go! Kim, who had been listening to Bob's side of the conversation, later said she thought we'd had a good talk. But I didn't remember anything good about it.

The crutch I had leaned on for the past four years and three months—my hope for a miracle cure—was being knocked out from under me. I was trying desperately to keep my sense of balance. My voice was strained, and I was fighting tears. I can't even remember what we said to each other. I finally realized how tired Bob was and how my wanting to try one more thing was just too much for him now. It was too late. He had already signed back into hospice.

"Stop it," he had told me. There was nothing more I could do. We had known from the beginning that it was terminal cancer. Searching for a cure had helped me avoid the inevitable for a long time, but now I had to face it. I had to admit that I hadn't been able to find a cure for my son. I wanted to believe I could accept God's will whatever it was, but I realized I just wasn't ready yet to accept Bob's death. I wanted that miracle!

I suddenly remembered my prayer at my youngest son's bedside in January of 1988 as he lay in a coma. I had felt compelled that evening to lay my hand on David and pray. I had asked for God to heal David, but I also prayed for God's will—whatever that might be. Had I really been willing back then to accept "whatever"? But God had healed one son; why wouldn't He do it again?

God is able to heal, and God can work miracles. I've seen it, and I still believe it. But not everyone is healed. God must have a purpose for whatever He allows, I told myself; but I wasn't ready to accept it. I felt so totally helpless.

I wished with all my heart that Bob had consented to another chemo treatment when the doctor had recommended it. He might have lived a little longer. But would it have stopped the cancer? Or would it have only prolonged his suffering? I wanted to trust God that everything had happened as it was supposed to happen—but I struggled with my uncertainties.

God does not interfere with men's choices or the consequences of man's actions. Bad things happen, and God does not stop them from happening. This world's diseases kill innocent people, and God allows it. I believe we have too many pollutants on this earth that can cause cancer.

Praying for strength and peace was my only option left. God had helped our family in many ways over the past four years. I had sensed His presence and His love many times, and I had seen His hand at work. I wanted to believe He was still in control.

Bob had two weeks. He said I could come, but he thought it would be too hard. He said he wanted to spend his last days with his family, to help Kim get ready. But wasn't I family? At first, I wondered if he didn't want me to come. That thought hurt deeply at first—but I understood what he meant.

I thought I should go, but I had to agree with Bob. It might be too hard. Truthfully, I was afraid to go. I didn't trust my own emotions, and I wasn't sure I could handle it. Bob and I had already said everything we needed to say to one another. My being with him now would not help him or the family. I held tight to the memory of the two days with Bob, two months earlier, when I had kissed his forehead and held his hand for the last time.

The waiting was agonizing, and my indecision made it worse. It may have been easier not to go, but I had to do something. I called a florist and arranged to send a small bouquet of flowers with a note. I would have sent bluebells, but they didn't have any.

Bob's final two texts, both the same, are still preserved on my cell phone: "Good morning! Love you!" I cannot, and I will not delete my son's last words dated one week before he died.

On Thursday morning, I woke up early. Russ was still asleep. I lay there quietly praying for God's strength and peace. I asked for His Spirit to be with Bob and Kim and the girls to help them through this heartbreaking time. It was nine days since Bob had called to tell me he had two weeks.

Silent words suddenly interrupted my prayer: "Bob will soon meet Jesus. He will have a new body, and a life free of pain." For a moment, I was stunned. And then an explosive wave of praise overwhelmed me. Yes, praise!

I've tried to relive that unexpected moment, but I can't. It was so incredibly personal. As I heard those words, I understood that Bob's eternal gain was more important than my loss. Bob was going to Heaven! He would have a new healthy body. He would stand straight and tall again, not bent over from spinal damage. No more pain. No more cancer. No more chemo or radiation treatments. He would be safe with Jesus in his Heavenly mansion.

God had answered my desperate prayers with a reminder that Bob's life would continue into a new dimension. For four years and three months, I had waited for a miracle of healing. I realized that eternal life is God's ultimate miracle.

His message of assurance gave me the comfort and strength I needed to get through those next few days. I felt God's love surrounding me and filling me even as the tears flowed. His loving presence was so real at that moment that it overshadowed everything else.

Three days later, Bob passed away peacefully in Kim's arms while the girls sang to him from the hallway—because Bob had not wanted them to see him go. With all the pain meds from hospice, I wondered later if he heard their song. I want to believe that God allowed him the blessing of that loving farewell.

Kim's call that Sunday afternoon surprised me. "Already?" I didn't say that word out loud, but I thought it. Funny how we react when we don't want to believe the news. I remember laughing out loud when I was told my dad died unexpectedly. Is that denial?

Bob died one month before his fiftieth birthday. One month before his twenty-fifth anniversary. Seven months after the mission trip to Nicaragua. Two months after the family came together on New Year's weekend.

I remembered the day that Bob had been born, prematurely. He had entered this world early—and now he had left too soon.

Part Two

THE AFTERMATH

SAYING GOODBYE

I'm sure Bob never imagined that four hundred people would come to say goodbye. He had planned his own memorial service, and Kim faithfully took care of all the details. She had wisely arranged for a much larger church than the one they attended.

For two hours, we celebrated memories of Bob's life. A slideshow moved through scenes from the forty-nine years that God had given him, and I remember feeling sadly glad to once again relive those times. I saw a picture of Bob as a happy little boy and photos of Bob with his brothers at different ages. A picture of Bob in a relay race at a school track meet. Bob in his high school graduation gown giving his valedictorian speech. Photos of his 4-H projects—Holstein cows and a palomino horse. Something reminded me that Bob had earned a sportsmanship trophy for patience when his dog Muffie didn't win the 4-H class. There were also photos from his college days when he met Kim. Later in the service we heard the CD with Bob's testimony, along with photos of his mission trip to Nicaragua with Alison.

All of Bob's girls participated in the service. Alison played her violin and sang a song she had written, accompanied by a friend on his guitar. The most difficult song for me, because I knew the story behind it, was when Alison, Hannah, and Sharon sang an unusual harmony piece they had named "Daddy's Lullaby." Hannah had arranged this song; it was the one that she and her sisters sang from the hallway while their daddy went to sleep in Kim's arms on his way to the Heavenly mansion where he lives today.

Sharon had painted her feelings onto a canvas, and she shared with us the meaning of each color. Her painting was on display near the stage along with two paintings Bob had done as therapy during his cancer years. One of his paintings had been copied from a vacation photo of a huge rocky mound along a California shore. Kim used that photo on the memorial handouts.

Bob had left his painting unfinished, however, without the three silhouetted figures of his girls pictured on top of the mound. His art instructor was able to complete that task the day before the service, and we all saw that as another evidence of God's grace.

Mark and David's words of tribute to their brother made me proud. Both had moments of emotional overflow, and I sat there wanting to give each one a hug. Mark told how he looked up to his younger brother. David shared moments from their years of growing up. We had lived in a thirteen-room farmhouse on four acres, with a big old barn. I smiled as I remembered the three boys at home and the work involved with their 4-H projects—David's chickens and Bob's and Mark's cows and horses. David mentioned Bob's tight-fisted ways, and everyone laughed because it was so well-known. Our laughter was a welcome momentary release from the tension of grief.

The last song of the program touched me most. Hannah, Sharon, and Alison were joined by their older sister, Ambre; and the four girls stood on stage in their lovely black dresses and sang a song called "Love." They shed some tears, and their voices broke; but they continued singing to the precious ending, "Life is brief, but when it's gone...love goes on and on..." How could it go on without Bob?

I couldn't imagine cancer being part of God's plan for Bob's life—until I later read a quote by Dr. Charles Stanley of In Touch ministries: "The only way to have conviction about the Lord's adequacy is to endure weakness, and then witness the strength that springs from it." I saw Bob's life as a living example of those words. I wondered if I could endure the way he had, and I hoped I would never have to. It was bad enough from a distance.

Bob's memorial service did something that I hadn't expected. Ever since leaving the father of my sons, I had seen myself as a failure. All three families had welcomed Russ and me together, but I struggled with guilt. Sometimes I felt like a sinner outside the fold—like I didn't really "belong" anymore. During the service, I became very aware that we were sharing Bob's loss as a family. We had always been a family in spite of my feelings.

Bob had brought us all together, even as he fought cancer. He had arranged the Florida vacation in June, the mission trip with Alison in July, and various visits with family members. On Valentine's Day, he had gone on a "date" with Kim and their three girls after learning he had two weeks to live. He left us with good memories of his love for family—and a very empty space in our lives.

That last weekend we were all together visiting Bob, we had talked about another family vacation. We knew his time was limited; perhaps we were simply pretending to keep up morale. Without Bob, it never happened. Without Bob, perhaps another family vacation would be too painful. I just believed that the rest of us would get together again somewhere, sometime; I didn't realize how different our lives would be.

One of my sons is gone from this Earth. I can no longer talk to him in person and hear his answering voice, but I know in my heart where he is. Quoting the words of a friend, Bob is now basking in the light of the loving presence of his Heavenly Father. But I believe we are all living in the light of His presence right here on this Earth; we only need to open our hearts to receive it. I realize that isn't as easy as it sounds.

Chapter Eleven

EASTER'S MESSAGE
PERSONALIZED

After saying our goodbyes, we returned to our homes. After being together in that emotionally intimate atmosphere, now we seemed terribly far apart. I learned why it's harder on loved ones after the services are over. It isn't just the loneliness of loss, however; it's also the questions that arise while dealing with the issue of death itself.

Three weeks after Bob's memorial service, we celebrated Easter—the death, burial, and resurrection of Jesus. Three weeks after saying goodbye to a son I believed to now be in Heaven, I was celebrating the very event that was the foundation of my belief. Did God possibly use this timing to bring new reality to Biblical truth?

God's Word tells us that Jesus rose from the dead three days after His crucifixion. His resurrection is our assurance that we will live in Heaven with Him. I had believed Scripture most of my life, but now my belief had been confirmed by prophetic words from God's Spirit three days before Bob died. Was it a coincidence—this additional occurrence of three days? Perhaps God arranges things to strengthen our faith. Even though He did not heal my son in answer to prayer, His message of assurance confirmed the Biblical message of Easter and made it extremely personal.

Without Christ's sacrifice on the cross, we would not have the hope of eternal life. Bob was in Heaven—because of Jesus! I was more thankful than ever for what Jesus had done on the cross and for what that meant to me and to our whole family.

I had known about Jesus since I was a little girl. Dad had always taken me to church, and he had taught me to pray. As a teenager, I had been confirmed in the Methodist Church; and I believed in one triune God—Father, Son, and Holy Spirit.

My experience with Bob's death added new depth to my understanding of the Easter message. I empathized with Mary's grief, knowing she had to watch her son die in such a heart-wrenching way. How could she possibly have understood the victory over death that would result from her son's terrible crucifixion? How could she have known that His sacrifice was the ultimate gift of God's love and that His resurrection would become God's message of hope to all believers?

In Matthew 28:20, Jesus told His disciples after his resurrection that He would always be with them, through His Spirit. I saw that He was with Bob through his years of struggle with cancer. He was with our whole family during our time of loss. Jesus kept His promise.

Believing His promise is the foundation of our faith. Learning to wholeheartedly trust God as we actually experience difficult times, however, is sometimes a challenge.

Chapter Twelve

TOPPLED

*A*fter Bob's death, Russ' love and support was a great comfort. I was also thankful for our little dog Lil; her playful antics still made me smile even when I didn't feel like smiling.

For three months, Lil's joyful personality often pushed aside my grief. One Sunday night in May, Lil went to the front door as usual right at six o'clock, asking to go out. I opened the door and watched her bouncy short-legged stride ploppity-plop down the porch steps. After using the same pee-spot as always, one foot from the sidewalk, she immediately came back to the porch steps.

This time, she stopped at the bottom stair and looked up. I watched as she bounced ploppity-plop back up those stairs and through the living room door as I held it open. Instead of running eagerly to her bed as usual, she stopped just inside the doorway. I remember that moment, as I wondered why she stopped. Russ called her, and she finally circled around the coffee table and went to him. He gave her the customary bedtime treat as she entered her crate, and he closed the door.

After an hour of resting quietly, she would usually make lots of frustrated doggie noises as she rearranged her blanket. We had always laughed at the way she fussed and struggled with that blanket as she tried to fix it just the way she wanted it. That night, we heard no fussing and no loud snoring. We were watching an exciting TV movie only a few feet from her crate. I walked past her several times on my way to the kitchen and back, and she seemed to be sleeping soundly.

At bedtime, we called her name to let her out one more time. But instead of the usual quick response, there was nothing. I opened the door of her crate and again spoke her name. I reached out to touch her—and I felt the cold stiffness of her body. I looked at Russ. His eyes showed the same disbelief that slowly overwhelmed me. I looked again at the motionless body in Lil's crate. That image still haunts me.

Russ and I stared at each other in shock. We held each other and cried; it was too late to do anything else. We finally went to bed, but I lay there awake until I realized why I couldn't sleep. I got up and carefully wrapped her body in her blanket, and then I took her out to the car and laid her gently beside my saddle in the trunk. I couldn't ask Russ to deal with it.

In the morning, I took Lil to be cremated. I drove the whole trip with the car windows open, surprised that the odor of her death had invaded everything inside the car. The next time I saddled Lady for a ride, she acted strangely nervous. I knew right away it was the smell that lingered on my saddle and its pad that had been stored in the trunk. I washed the pad, and I cleaned the saddle. The odor hung on still, a lingering reminder of the sadness of our loss. We traded the car off sooner than planned.

Before Lil's death, I had been quite proud of myself; I believed I was handling Bob's passing better than most mourning mothers I knew. After all, I had God's words of assurance, my husband's understanding, and a dog to make me smile. And then Lil's unexpected death completely toppled me. For some reason, I thought of the three-legged stool my dad had used when milking, and I realized that one leg of my support system was gone.

It was too soon after losing Bob. My grief was magnified seemingly beyond reason. Was I crying more for a dog than I had for my precious son? At first, I couldn't understand; but I'd had years to prepare for Bob's death, and I had grieved my share of tears along the way. The shock of losing Lil so unexpectedly, right there in our living room, was difficult to absorb. I was suddenly grateful that I hadn't been with Bob when he died.

Perhaps the agony of Bob's loss was less acute because of some slight relief; at least his struggle with pain was over. I remembered feeling similar relief after my dad died—relief that he was no longer alone and I wouldn't have to worry about his health and safety. I knew he was in Heaven.

Lil died nine days before her ninth birthday. Like Bob, she died too young. She'd had an operation four months earlier due to bladder problems, but that surely wouldn't have caused her death, we thought. Was it a heart attack? A stroke? It could have been either one. Russ thought she had been acting old for a few days. Maybe I didn't see the signs because I was so focused on my loss of a son. Could we have saved Lil if we had known something was wrong? Her loss was simply one more question left unanswered.

Two weeks after Lil's death, I found a dog's small tooth on the carpet in front of the TV. That very day, I read a Facebook post that said if you find a memento from a departed pet, it was thinking of you. That sounded nice, but I didn't really believe it. I had taken Lil's crate out to clean it, I remembered, so the tooth probably had fallen out of the crate then. Her tooth is still on my kitchen windowsill—a treasured parting gift from a little dog with scars on her back and love in her heart, a dog who had meant so much to both of us.

Chapter Thirteen

A CARDINAL'S MESSAGE

*I*f I believed in mystical messages, I would say we'd been warned about Lil's death; but it was years later before I learned about the superstitious belief that a bird flying into a window is a bad omen.

Lil died on a Sunday evening. The previous Friday morning, I'd been awakened by knocking sounds; and I had entered the living room to see a male cardinal flying into the front picture window. Knowing the feisty red bird is notorious for attacking his image—and not yet knowing about the superstition—I was amused. I watched his crazy antics, and I took a video.

Saturday morning, the cardinal again woke me. I watched as he flew into the window, sang his loud cheery song from the porch railing, and again flew at the window. I was afraid he would hurt himself. Was it really a coincidence that the cardinal appeared three days before Lil died?

When I posted my video on Facebook, a friend commented that she saw a single male cardinal as a symbol of the Holy Spirit, and we should feel blessed. She also said, "When we experience loss, God fills our empty spaces with new blessings." Those words brought tears. Really? Was this persistent cardinal possibly a blessing from above?

My grandmother had loved cardinals. One had sung in the tree above us during the prayer at her graveside service. His loud "What cheer, what-what-what?" had almost drowned out the minister's words. Family members later agreed it was surely the same cardinal that Grandma and my dad had fed every morning at their home only a mile from the cemetery. Dad continued to feed the birds until he died eight years later.

My visiting cardinal came day after day, to fly into the window. I was sure he was seeing his reflection, thinking it was another male. It was breeding season, and he was simply defending his territory. I lowered the blinds, hoping he wouldn't see his reflection.

THE PERSISTENT CARDINAL AT THE WINDOW

A month later, there was a banging sound at the back door early one morning. I knew it was the cardinal. When I opened the door, he flew up onto a nearby tree branch singing loudly. Was he waking me up to bless me with his cheery song?

For a week, I was awakened every morning by that cardinal banging on the back door or the patio glass doors. I didn't get up. It was no longer amusing. I wanted to shout, "Go away! Let me sleep!"

My friend's Facebook post about the cardinal being a symbol of the Holy Spirit made me wonder, though. If this persistent cardinal was a blessing from above, was there a message connected to his behavior? Could there be some spiritual reason for his visits?

A well-known painting of Jesus shows him knocking on a cottage door—a symbol of His knocking on the door of our hearts. Did the cardinal's visits symbolize the Holy Spirit wanting entry into our home? As I awoke each morning, I prayed He would come in and bless us with His enabling power.

I remembered my healing experience thirty-five years earlier during my first marriage, when God's Spirit had touched me. While visiting in a town where I once worked, I had decided to go to my former employer's office—just because his wife had jotted a note in their Christmas card that he was now doing marriage counseling. I respected Roy's judgment, and I wanted his advice because I was considering a divorce.

I didn't have an appointment, but when Roy saw me enter the building he immediately waved at me to invite me into his office. I had just sat down opposite his desk when a stranger opened the door. He told us he was driving through town and thought he was supposed to stop. "Is there some need here?" Roy didn't believe in coincidences. I remember he chuckled and pointed to me, "You probably need to talk to this lady."

Who was this man, I wondered, and what did he need to talk about?

Three hours later, I left Roy's office feeling very different than when I had entered. Apparently, God had sent the stranger to heal my spinal condition. Several years earlier I had sneezed with my head turned while loading clothes into the dryer. After that, I had been bucked off a horse. I'd also suffered a whiplash when a car hit me from behind at a stop sign. I had been going to chiropractors for relief, but my problem was getting worse. We lived on an acreage at the time, with a big garden and chickens, cows, and horses—and I wasn't able to carry a bucket of water without pain.

The stranger talked to me and prayed for me, and then he told me that God wanted to heal me. I had never thought to pray for healing for my neck and back; it wasn't a life threatening problem, and I'd been more focused on praying for my unhappy marriage. But before I left Roy's office, I knew I'd been healed. Walking felt different, like it does after a chiropractic adjustment. I never did ask Roy for marriage advice that day, but an experience several weeks later convinced me that God had stepped in with His own answer.

My husband and I were back together after a six month separation. We were talking in the laundry room when he suddenly started screaming at me. That wasn't unusual, but it always caught me by surprise. Usually I would have yelled back at him or run to the bedroom in tears. This time, for the very first time, I heard his frustration; and I stood there quietly listening.

I later realized that God's Spirit had responded to my husband through me as I had never been able to do on my own. It was an awesome, humbling experience. A stranger had touched me with physical healing, and I now was able to do chores without pain. I no longer needed to go to a chiropractor. I also felt spiritually cleansed and filled with the power of the Holy Spirit, and His enabling influence was helping me deal with my marriage in new ways.

For several months, I was often aware of the Spirit working through me. I believed I had found the secret to living the Christian life, but I remember feeling a pride in my new life that gradually pushed aside my dependence on God's Spirit.

There is more to the story, beyond the scope of this memoir. Our marriage relationship still had its problems—the way humans always have problems when we depend on our own human wisdom more than God's guidance. Twenty-five years later, we agreed on a divorce.

Not long after my experience in Roy's office, I asked God why He would heal me instead of fixing my marriage. I was thankful for the miraculous healing, but I had prayed for my marriage for eighteen years! I wasn't afraid to ask God questions, even though I didn't always get answers. This time He led me to Matthew 9:6 (NIV), "...that you may know that the Son of Man has authority on earth to forgive sins..."

Didn't I already know that? When I had accepted Christ, my awareness of His forgiveness was a memorable experience. Life's struggles since then, however, had made me wonder where I stood. Feelings of unworthiness had created doubt.

I was trying to be a good person, even though I knew that human goodness was not the key to Heaven. I knew that my forgiveness was based only on my faith in Jesus—because He was the One who died on the cross for me. I trusted in His grace and His righteousness, not my own. Grace is His unconditional love even when I don't deserve it. Like many others, I was trying to live the Christian life from my own resources. That does not work; we are authentic Christians only when Christ lives in us through His Spirit.

I think God knew I would someday feel the burden of my human weakness, and He gave me words from Scripture that I would remember the rest of my life. I needed to learn again and again to depend on His strength!

Had the cardinal come to remind me how God's Spirit had worked in my life in the past? I remembered my awareness of His enabling, and I longed to have that awareness again. Did I need another healing touch?

Morning after morning the cardinal flew into the front window or the back door or the patio door, waking me up, getting me up until I believed there had to be a reason beyond his bird brain obsession. In a way, I was thankful for the cardinal's persistence. I wanted to believe it symbolized the Spirit's desire to fill me with His power, and I didn't want Him to give up on me. But I still worried the bird could get hurt, and I was still frustrated by his wake up calls so early each morning!

Hoping to distract him, I tried putting sunflower seeds out in a feeder. I taped newspaper on the inside of the back door. Then I taped newspaper on the inside of the sliding patio doors. He flew into any places I missed, so I added more newspaper until every inch of glass was covered.

After two months of the cardinal's early noise, I finally woke up to silence. I actually missed those morning wake-up calls just as I missed our precious Lil's insistent demands for attention. At least the cardinal's crazy antics had taken my mind off my losses. He had filled my empty place with a strange blessing.

Before Lil came, I had often enjoyed morning quiet times sitting alone in our back yard by the lake. After we had Lil, I was busy with her morning needs. Now she was gone. The cardinal had awakened me, and I had no excuse. I decided to return to those quiet moments with God. I wanted to find once again that greater awareness of His presence in my daily life!

Because of a persistent cardinal, I again sat by the lake in the early mornings to meditate and to be still before God. I sat there and read my devotional guide, and I prayed. I remembered how God had blessed me in the past. I prayed for guidance to once again experience the influence of His Spirit. The quiet peace of the morning comforted me, and the water of the lake was a soothing landscape. My visiting cardinal often sang from a tree branch above me; perhaps he was singing to celebrate the delivery of his message.

DEALING WITH GRIEF IN STAGES

When I asked Hannah, one of my twin granddaughters, how Kim and the other girls were doing, she replied that each one was dealing with grief in her own way.

For a year after Bob died, Kim ran from facing her pain by traveling and visiting friends and relatives, while driving the new car Bob had purchased not long before he died. Perhaps she was avoiding the loneliness of the home she and Bob had shared for almost twenty-five years, or perhaps she simply felt the need for support from others.

With Bob gone and Kim traveling, the three girls left home one by one to pursue their dreams. It was time. They had stayed in order to be with their dad as long as possible. Now, Facebook posts were often my only news of their activities. I saw photos of Sharon enjoying her glamorous modeling career as she traveled to New York and Paris. I learned that Hannah was questioning her future as a beautician. Alison was finding comfort in her relationship with a fellow musician, the one who had accompanied her at Bob's memorial service.

Before my divorce, our whole family had met together several times a year in our home. After the divorce, Bob's home became our central meeting place. With everyone now scattered apart, we no longer had a central "home." I was overcome with loss of not only a son, but of the togetherness of a family. It broke my heart to know that my family would never be the same again. I sometimes wished that Russ and I had a larger place with more room for everyone.

With Bob gone, I craved more contact with Mark and David. I missed my boys, but I couldn't tell them how much; I didn't want to be a needy mother. They were busy with their office jobs and their own families, and I was sure they needed time alone to heal, just as I did. Mark was miles away in California, and he worked long hours. David later moved to Chicago, and his job sometimes brought him to our area. I was very happy to see him whenever he could come.

Counselors name five stages of grief, but the process is always different for everyone who grieves. Those five basic stages—denial, bargaining, depression, anger and acceptance—do not follow a set schedule. It takes as long as it takes to work through them, and you can't hurry the process. We all knew Kim was trying to avoid her grief, and I wondered when it would catch up with her. I was glad she found a good counselor who helped her through the process.

My own grief didn't worry me at first. I assumed my Christian faith would get me through this loss, just as it had gotten me through the losses of my dad, my grandparents, and others. This painful wound would heal, I believed, and I would get on with life. But some wounds are deeper than others, and some healings take longer. Discovering that truth for myself was a surprise. Kim reminded me one day, "You've never lost a son before."

Even though I knew that God had lovingly moved Bob from a painful earthly home to a glorious Heavenly mansion, a part of me deep within my mother's heart still reached out for him. But my little boy had grown up and left my world for another dimension.

I've known some mothers who never got over such a loss, and I was determined to not let that happen to me. I turned to Jeremiah 29:11-13 (NIV). "For I know the plans I have for you," declares the

Lord, "plans to prosper you and not to harm you, plans to give you a hope and a future." Bob's life on earth was over, but mine wasn't. I wanted to honor Bob's memory by living my life with the same faith I saw in him. I wanted to help the rest of our family remember all that God had done for us—by writing my memoir.

Horses had been my greatest passion since childhood, and riding had often been my escape from unhappiness. Russ had given his old mare away and quit riding, so we no longer trailered our horses to scenic park trails. I had lost Traveller to EPM, and I had sold Rocky. Lady, my Tennessee Walking Horse, was now my only riding partner. The year that Bob died, I rode more than ever.

Lady wasn't as calm as Traveller had been when ridden without the company of other horses, however, and I missed the horse that had taken such good care of me. A goal gives energy and purpose, and that's what I needed! So I decided to see how far I could ride Lady alone outside the boarding stable. Besides the outdoor arena, there was a path along a drainage ditch that led to five acres of woods. There were also fields nearby and the road in front of the stable.

The trail back to the woods seemed safer, since I didn't have the confidence to go too far beyond Lady's comfort zone. I'd done that once before, our first trip down the road. She had spun with me when a big noisy dump truck passed. Years later, fears of riding on that road still plagued me.

At first, we went a very short distance on the trail. I wanted Lady to relax and enjoy our rides, so I stopped often to let her eat grass. I rode only where I felt safe. Going a little further each ride, we gradually made our way through the winding trails inside the wooded area. It took me two weeks to ease her through a "scary" tree-lined narrow passageway between fields until she went through with calm acceptance. I was proud of what I did with her that year, and my confidence grew as I worked on hers. Riding Lady helped me work in the present instead of grieving the past.

In September, I experienced a setback. As I emptied a very full muck bucket into a manure spreader, I felt a sharp pain at my wrist; I had sprained a tendon. That simple injury was the first step toward a life-changing decision. Movement was painful whenever I tried to lift a saddle or clean Lady's stall. I stopped riding, expecting to resume in the spring. It was discouraging to put aside my passion.

I've heard people say, "When God closes one door, He opens another." I agree that He seems to bless me with something new whenever it's time to let go of the old. I see His blessings as gifts to show His love or care. I believe blessings have the power to keep us going through difficult times.

Lil's happy, loving personality had been a blessing. Riding Lady had been a blessing. In the past, God had blessed me through many different horses and dogs, as well as through nature, music, people, and Scripture. I believe He works through our experiences and interests to teach us lessons we might not learn otherwise. Through my relationships with horses, I had found a deeper understanding of how He works in my life; and I had often sensed His involvement in my experiences. But now, it seemed as though my blessings were slipping away.

Chapter Fifteen

SMALL COMFORT;
BIG CHALLENGE!

Russ and I had agreed we never wanted another dog. We knew that no other dog could ever take Lil's place. But I saw how he missed her. I missed her too. She had been a daily part of our lives for three and a half years. On those nights when I lay in bed awake, I still listened for her snoring.

As I ate my breakfast, I no longer shared my banana with Lil. I missed the entertainment of playing with her. I missed her little paws digging at my leg for attention. I missed her lying at my feet in my office as I wrote my columns. I missed her demanding, fun-loving personality. Would another dog be a small comfort?

One day, I began to look at rescue dogs online. One dog looked so much like Lil that I cried out loud in surprise. Of course it wasn't Lil. None of them were Lil. But now I couldn't stop looking. I emailed the three people who had known our dog—the breeder, the veterinarian, and the couple who gave her to us. The breeder emailed back that she had a three-year-old Boston terrier she wanted to retire from breeding. Was it fair to another dog to expect her to fill the deep hole that Lil's passing had left in our lives?

Hoping for an answer, we drove several hours to see the breeder's dog. Her registered name was "Motif's She Wore a Yellow Ribbon." They called her "Ribbons." I got down on my knees to get acquainted, but she looked so much like her parents and sister that I couldn't tell them apart. When the breeder told Ribbons to give me a kiss, she came and touched my cheek gently with her little red tongue. Such a sweet dog, I thought.

She didn't look or act like Lil. Although both dogs had been born in this same breeder's home, they were from different bloodlines. Lil's demanding, playful personality was the opposite of Ribbons' sensitive, quiet nature. Lil had seemed eager to be our only dog. Ribbons was hesitant. But Ribbons fit our requirements, and she was available. We decided to buy her.

We brought Ribbons home on a Wednesday in early August of 2013. I took her out several times a day, but she held everything in until Thursday afternoon. We returned from lunch to find her complete deposit on the carpet in front of the TV, and I found her under the coffee table, trembling. The breeder had assured us that Ribbons was completely house broken. So how did this happen? Why didn't she go in the yard when I gave her the chance?

I remembered that Ribbons had been trained to do her business only in her own fenced back yard. Was she so well trained that she couldn't adapt? The breeder had said that her dogs often held it for long periods when they were away from home at a dog show. She had also said that Ribbons was very conscientious, and she would be broken hearted if she thought she had done something wrong. I was so sorry for this dog now trembling under the coffee table. I didn't have the heart to punish her, knowing she had held it for twenty-seven hours—perhaps waiting to get home to her own familiar fenced yard.

At first, I saw Ribbons as a timid dog. If someone knocked on the door, she ran for the kitchen. Lil would have barked ferociously! Russ swatted a fly in the living room one day, and Ribbons paced back and forth in the kitchen, refusing to eat her supper. She didn't play with toys or chew on the bone that came with her. She didn't bark. She didn't do much of anything except sleep under our huge coffee table. Lil had sometimes slept there, so perhaps Ribbons was comforted by the smell of dog.

Information I found online said to never look directly at a timid dog. Yet when I told Ribbons to "go poop," she would stare directly at me for a long time without doing anything. It frustrated me!

Why didn't I see the pleading sadness within those chocolaty brown eyes with their central depth of dark blue? I should have understood sooner. I had lost a son; but Ribbons had lost her parents, a sister, and the company of other dogs, as well as the people who cared for her. She had lost the only home she knew, and now she found herself suddenly alone with new people in a strange place. She didn't even know where to relieve herself.

Was she really timid—or was it the lonely uncertainty of the change in homes? We felt sad about taking her away from her former comfort.

WHAT DO HER EYES TELL YOU?

It was Russ who first saw how Ribbons and I were much alike. "Smart and curious," he said, "but quiet, sensitive, and cautious." I'd always wished I was more decisive, like Russ. Lady and Lil were also fast thinkers; but like Ribbons, I took longer to consider options. I agreed that our personalities were very similar.

Early training leaves a strong imprint, and Ribbons and I both had strict upbringing. Ribbons had been trained to respect exact physical boundaries—to relieve herself only within a certain fenced back yard. With no fences in our small yard, she seemed confused.

I had been trained to respect the acceptable behaviors set forth by church and family. When I was born, Mother and Dad lived with his parents on a rented farm, and Dad helped with the work. Grandpa and Grandma Moats had a strong faith, and Grandpa's strict beliefs left little room for compromise. My parents' marriage, hastened by Mother's pregnancy, had not met Grandpa's expectations.

After three years of living with Grandpa's judgmental attitude, my mother walked away. I grew up without her, and I felt "different" because I had no mother and no memory of her. Her absence was a silent mystery. No one would talk about her or what had happened, and I was afraid to ask questions. That cloud of uncertainty hung over my head until I was in my late twenties.

My mother found me after Grandpa died, and I finally heard her side of the story. Her painful past had left scars, and our relationship was never what I'd hoped for. I've often heard that you can't go back. It's true.

Do strong feelings from the past stay with us all our lives? Was I still a captive to the uncertainty I'd known as a youngster, and did that uncertainty cause my grownup cautious indecision? How could I get over it?

Similarities between me and Ribbons went even further, as I thought about it. She probably felt out of place in her new home with no other dogs, just as I had felt in my first marriage when I was the only female with four males. My husband did not know how to treat a woman with love and respect. Once, he jokingly said I wasn't worth it. One counselor warned us that our relationship was detrimental to our whole family. I kept looking for someone to fix it, because I wasn't sure how to stand up for myself without starting an argument. Compared to Lil's persistent, demanding personality, I saw how much Ribbons and I had in common. I tried to make her feel loved and accepted the way I would have wanted.

Like Ribbons, I spent most of my life afraid that I would do something wrong. When I was young, I had tried very hard to be a good little girl. When I was older, I wanted to be a good wife, a good mother, a good Christian woman. I had grown up in a family that saw divorce as something so shameful that it was kept secret from a little girl. Or perhaps it was the forced marriage as much as the divorce that caused the shame. Since we could never talk about it, I wasn't sure. It took a great deal of courage for me to finally give up on my first marriage—to defy my belief that I was a good Christian as long as I stayed. For both Mother and me, divorce seemed the only escape from our misery.

In spite of the uncertainty, I am still grateful for the genuine love of my dad and grandparents who raised me. I am thankful for their Godly influence. I'm also thankful that I'm learning about the freedom within God's grace.

When my friendship with Russ developed into a romantic adventure, my guilt was a constant burden. Change can be difficult for both dogs and people. Hopefully, we can adapt without losing the important principles we learned at an early age. Russ and I have been blessed beyond all my expectations, and I feel more loved than ever before.

Chapter Sixteen

FINDING A NEW PATH

Ribbons was supposed to be a comforting companion, snuggling on the sofa with us as we enjoyed her adorable kisses. Although she was a sweet dog—attentive, well trained, and very polite—her unexpected response to a change in homes was frustrating. I realized I would have to literally retrain this dog to relieve herself in a new place.

It was a time-consuming process. I was no expert on dog training, and I soon became aware that my grief did not enhance my patience. There was a silver lining, however—working with Ribbons focused my attention on something beyond my grief. Perhaps I needed that. God often gives us what we need instead of what we think we want.

The grassy area that I could see from our front porch, the area where children play and residents walk their dogs, was the best place to start. It's a short hike across the road in front of our home, over two empty mobile home pads to the road in front of the grassy area. Friday morning I took Ribbons there, hoping for a breakthrough. Nothing happened. Following park rules, I had kept her on a leash. I didn't want her to run away and get lost.

By Saturday morning she had actually held it for forty hours since Thursday's deposit on the carpet. In sheer desperation, I took her to the grassy area and turned her loose. She went a distance away, did everything she was supposed to do, and then she joyously ran back to me. Aren't all dogs able to relieve themselves while on a leash? Had she been trained otherwise? I wish I had known!

Monday morning, five days after bringing Ribbons home, I took her out without a leash. She peed in the yard for the first time, and I lavished her with praise! After waiting a reasonable time, I took her on the leash to the grassy area. When I turned her loose, she finished her business.

That was when I noticed the newly mowed pathway into the adjoining field. Until a few years before, the field had been farmland planted in winter wheat or soybeans; and the property line between field and grassy area had been marked only by one tall mulberry tree surrounded by bushes and weeds.

One day in May of 2011, the mulberry tree was suddenly a pile of brush. The pile soon disappeared, and a long mound of dirt slowly formed along the property line. Over the finished berm, I could see the tops of heavy equipment moving back and forth. I was curious, but I was more concerned with my son's cancer than with what unknown people were doing in a hidden field.

Now that a newly mowed pathway led into the field, I wanted to see what the heavy equipment had done there. As I passed through the entrance between several feet of tall weeds and low thorny bushes on each side, two small, dark blue birds flew up—a pair of Indigo Buntings! Reaching the end of the high weedy entrance, I looked out at an open space of grass and weeds bordered by tall trees. It was the same field previously planted in crops—nothing special that I could see. Was all that heavy equipment only to build the berm that hid the field from view? Why hide it?

Ribbons and I stood for a moment looking around, but I went no farther that first morning. Not knowing yet who owned this field, I didn't want to be trespassing. I was sure Ribbons was as hungry for breakfast as I was; it was time to head for home. We would return another day.

It made me sad that she spent so much time under the coffee table. One day after lunch, I coaxed her out with a piece of salmon. Her eager response convinced me to buy some dog treats. I had an idea how to retrain this new dog!

Using those treats, I worked to change Ribbons' place of business from the grassy area to our yard. While she was off the leash in the grassy area, I taught her to sit, stay, and come; and I gave treats for obedience. Each time she relieved herself in our yard, she got a treat. After a few weeks, she was using our back yard on a regular basis instead of the park's grassy area.

Only once did I punish her for pooping in the house. When I found it on the carpet in my office one morning, I decided I had been too lenient. She needed to learn my rules. I took her back to the scene of her mistake. I firmly told her, "This is a no-no," and I gave her one gentle pat on her behind. Honestly, it was a very gentle pat because I knew she was especially sensitive. Her eyes opened wide, and she froze in place for such a long time that it scared me. And then she whirled and ran into the living room and dived under the coffee table. She hasn't come into my office since that day even though I've tried to coax her. But she hasn't had another accident in the house.

Fortunately, she hasn't held it against me. Russ and I spend evenings on the sofa watching TV, and Ribbons often sleeps close beside me on her blanket. I remember how she would sometimes inch closer and put her paws on my leg. I wondered if she was seeking the same comforting companionship I had hoped for. "She really loves you," Russ would tell me. Now, she sometimes lies against me so I can rub her tummy.

Chapter Seventeen

A CONNECTION WITH NATURE

*T*hrough the years, I've sometimes seen God arrange ordinary details to lead me to a certain path in life—or to a certain place where He could better reach me with the truth of His love. My pilgrimage into the secluded field near our mobile home park was one of those times.

Did God actually arrange for us to get just the right dog to lead me to a newly mowed pathway into a certain field? I believe it's possible. Ribbons was the perfect companion for my walks in that open field as I struggled to deal with the loss of my son. I didn't realize that walking the dog would become so much more.

Growing up on an Iowa farm, I had always loved dogs and nature; and I had spent many hours in our thirty-five acre wooded pasture. Our milk cows did not have a lush green meadow; they foraged for grass wherever it grew, from a few level grassy areas to the wooded hillsides and a steep ravine. I enjoyed my walks among the trees, hearing the scolding of squirrels or the call of a woodpecker, or listening to the gentle whisper of leaves fluttering in a summer breeze. I can still smell the spring fragrance of plum trees in blossom and hear the buzzing of visiting honey bees. I remember standing within a grove of sugar maple trees in autumn as their golden glow saturated my being.

My grandmother and I walked those woods in the spring to gather Morel mushrooms and wildflowers. In the fall, we picked berries for dinner and bittersweet for table decorations. If the cows were late coming home at night for milking, I enjoyed a grand adventure riding one of Grandpa's team of Percherons to go after them. I loved those woods. There, I was alone in my own private world of nature and make-believe. As I roamed that wooded pasture, my mind searched for answers to life's questions. Now God had led me into a different private world of nature where I could seek answers to new questions.

Because Bob died on February twenty-fourth, the twenty-fourth of each month became a day of remembrance. I found myself shedding tears on each one of those days as I thought about the son who was no longer here. Did it help to mark the steps away from that day of loss? Did it help to count the months?

When I began to walk the field with Ribbons, I'd counted six remembrance days. As I glanced at the calendar one day, I realized that it was the twenty-sixth. My "Remembrance Day" had passed by unnoticed for the first time. My grief was beginning to heal, which was surely a good thing; but I felt sad, as though I had lost even the precious observance of my son's memory. I wanted peace and healing, but how could I lose the grief without losing the only thing left of him—those memories that I embraced so desperately?

Then somewhere I read these words: "The loss is always with you, inside of you. But the person he was, the son you had, is also there." Those words impressed me with new understanding. I could visualize memories of Bob still lingering within my heart and mind, definitely not the same as his physical presence; but he was still with me, and I would never lose that part of him. I thought of Bob often as I walked the field with Ribbons, and God changed this journey of sadness into a pilgrimage of healing.

From an online website, I learned that the field was being

restored to its original state as an American Bottom wetland "for educational and recreational opportunities" for this Illinois community. The project was a combined effort of three groups: the Collinsville Area Recreational District, Madison County, and Heartlands Conservancy.

My first walk into the field revealed only the beginning of the project. From the entrance carved out between high weeds, I emerged to a divided trail. I could go straight or turn left. I chose to go straight ahead toward the distant trees.

The mowed pathway was comfortably wide with a sparseness of grass emerging from the sandy soil. The field itself was nothing but weeds and grasses, brightened in places along the path with a few stalks of yellow flowers in fragrant blossom. I recognized them as Partridge Pea, a legume I remembered from a high school class trip into a field near the small Iowa town where I grew up.

After a short ways, the trail sloped downward toward the line of trees. Just within the morning shade of those trees was a small man-made pond, almost hidden from view by cattails and surrounding grasses. Most likely, heavy equipment had dug the hole for this pond, using the same dirt to form the berm.

The mowed pathway that divided a few feet from the entrance was actually one circular path around the center of the field. Bordered by tall trees on three sides and the berm that separated it from the mobile home park's grassy area in front, the field was delightfully private.

This field once used as farmland was now a part of the new Arlington Wetlands. It was named for Arlington Drive where a special permeable parking lot was being built. I knew the area; I drove that road every day on my way to the boarding stable three miles away where my Lady was kept.

Between the new parking lot and the field where I walked was a long swampy lake sandwiched between tall trees. To connect the parking lot to the field, volunteers were building a white floating boardwalk resting just above the shallow water. Complete with handrails, it was the longest floating boardwalk in Southern Illinois, according to the website. Since the completion of the boardwalk in the fall of 2013, the entire wetlands area has been open to residents on both sides—those living along Arlington Drive as well as those in the mobile home park.

THE FLOATING BOARDWALK

When Ribbons and I first came to the boardwalk, she hesitated to walk onto the unusual white surface; I had to get down on her level and coax her to follow me. A large square platform at the center of the boardwalk made a convenient place to stand and look out over the shallow water in all directions, to "experience the swampy wetlands up close," quoting the Arlington Wetlands website. A generous growth of aquatic plants called yellow pond-lilies lifted their heart shaped leaves above the water's surface. I could see the bottom of their stems in the shallow water.

Looking north from the boardwalk, I saw a few of the homes along Arlington Drive. On my right, a short path through the trees led to the parking lot on Arlington Drive. On my left, the path led into the field where I walked Ribbons. As I looked south, the tree-lined, plant-filled swampy lake stretched out before me almost a mile to Horseshoe Lake Road, the same road that passed in front of our mobile home park.

LOOKING SOUTH FROM THE BOARDWALK

As I stood on the center of the boardwalk, I suddenly remembered the swans. For the past few years, a pair of mute swans had nested along the edge of this swampy water, closer to Horseshoe Lake Road. That last year there had been three little cygnets. Only one survived, the other two presumably victims of turtles that often grab young water babies from underneath.

Nature has many stories to tell and many lessons about life and death if we only take time to watch and listen. Nature's reality is often harsh. It is a food chain system where ants make dead worms disappear, where cats kill beautiful songbirds, and where turtles feast on water babies. As disturbing as it is, death is part of the system just as death is a natural outcome of mortal existence. I don't mind a blue heron or an eagle killing a fish for its breakfast. I don't want to watch. But I am disturbed about a turtle killing a little cygnet swan. Nature seems cruel at times, especially when death comes to something so magnificent. I prefer nature's gentle, natural beauty.

When the surviving young swan was old enough to fly, his parents brought him to visit our lake next door. When he came alone one day, I threw bread out on the water for him. Although I never touched him, I thought of him as my pet—this beautiful huge white bird so graceful and wild—because he would come to me when I called to him. I knew he came for the bread. I called him Henry, for lack of a better name.

MY BEAUTIFUL SWAN, HENRY

One day after he had eaten the bread from the water, he came out of the lake to stand beside me in our back yard. I told him that I didn't have any more bread, and he went back into the water. Of course I don't think he understood my words, but it was a treasured, mystical moment. One day I heard the loud throbbing, mechanical beating of his powerful wings as he flew away. That sound was a thrill I have never forgotten.

One year before Russ and I were married, he had purchased a more spacious house in town while planning to sell his mobile home. Since it didn't sell in that year, we decided to sell the house in town instead.

This is definitely home. It has been a safe place with good neighbors. We often sit in the back yard by the lake and relax while enjoying the peaceful setting. I have watched magnificent sunsets, and I've delighted in the changing colors and cloud formations. I've also seen and heard many different kinds of birds, and I've searched through my bird books to identify them. I enjoy taking photos of the birds, and I often use those photos to help with identification.

I have sensed an unusually personal connection with all of my surroundings here—our own Edelhardt Lake, the wetland lake, the trees, the birds, and especially the secluded field—all of this beauty of nature within walking distance. I feel a connection to God here. Knowing my love of nature, perhaps He worked it out to keep us in this lakeside mobile home.

Part Three

A PILGRIMAGE
OF HEALING

Chapter Eighteen

ARLINGTON WETLANDS

*O*n September of 2013, a few weeks after I discovered the newly mowed pathway, the Arlington Wetlands project officially opened to the public. It included three areas: the parking lot on Arlington Road between sections of natural grassland, the swampy lake spanned by the new boardwalk, and the adjoining field with its winding pathway and pond.

The field became my favorite place to explore, and I always took Ribbons with me. She needed the exercise, and she enjoyed our times in the field. When I asked if she wanted to go for a walk, she would often hop off the sofa and run to me, eagerly jumping up on my knee.

Our walks to the field were not a daily ritual; but for that fall of 2013 and all of 2014, it was my fascination. Whenever the weather was nice, we would go to the field. Sometimes we went early in the morning, when the dew left beads on the grass and the spider webs looked white in the sunlight. Sometimes it was later in the day. Whenever we walked the field, I saw something of beauty.

MORNING DEW ON GRASS

The new developments within the field interested me. Signs along the path told me about the wetlands. One near the pond explained how such areas provide protection from flooding. Wetlands also provide habitat for certain wildlife, including snakes, frogs, and turtles. The Arlington Wetlands project was an attempt to restore some of the wetlands that man had destroyed and to educate the public about their importance. We live under nature's rules—the principles that God established at creation—and when we try to ignore those rules, we have much to lose.

Another sign shows a map of North America with marked flyways of migrating birds. Our area, the Mississippi Flyway, is one of four natural travel paths that provide migrating birds with places for rest, food, and water as well as nesting and breeding. Scripture tells us that God takes care of His creation, and I see these flyways as examples of God's provision. I'm glad someone is working to keep such places available.

I already knew about the migrating white pelicans that come through this area each March and October—ever since my friend

Pam had identified the birds I'd seen while horseback riding. Pam was the same friend whose medical experience had been so helpful during my son David's liver transplant. She was also an experienced bird watcher and nature lover, and she wrote a newspaper column on wildlife. I had eagerly read her columns long before I met her the day she visited the office where I worked. The moment I heard her say her name to the receptionist, I became as excited as a teenager meeting a movie star!

We went out to lunch to get acquainted, and I learned she owned horses. When I told her the problems I was having with my new mare, she offered to help train Fanny that summer. With so many mutual interests, the special friendship born that day lasted for thirty years.

Whenever I saw the pelicans, I would call Pam to share my excitement. I might happen to see them as we were driving to lunch or while at the stable where we boarded our horses. Suddenly, unexpectedly, I would see a flock of them swirling in graceful circles in the sky. I loved to watch them for as long as possible, fascinated by their synchronized movements. As they circled, sometimes the sun would catch the black tips of their white wings, and sometimes they seemed to disappear in the sunlight's brightness. I always thanked God for each sighting, as if He allowed it for a special surprise just for me.

Pam and I could talk for hours—about horses, about birds and nature, and about life. I wished I could tell Pam about the Arlington Wetlands, but she had died of leukemia six years before I discovered this place. She hadn't even told me she was sick, if she knew; I thought she was tired from working long hours. When I hadn't heard from her for two weeks, which was unusual, I called her. I was informed that she was in the hospital, unresponsive. And then she was gone—a few days before her sixty-first birthday.

Pam died the year before Bob was diagnosed with cancer. I missed having her help during my crisis. That sounds selfish; but she knew a lot about cancer, and her advice would have been valuable.

Ever since we met and she helped me train my first horse, I always turned to Pam when I had a problem. She usually had an answer to almost any question. Even though she was seven years younger than I was, I looked up to her. I believed I needed her. She had the confidence I lacked, and she helped me face the hard times. She could often explain my feelings before I could put them into words. We had a spiritual friendship that was unusually close.

She once confided that she didn't have many friends. She was too controlling, some thought, but I understood she had an inner need to be a caretaker. When helping others, she tended to take over and do more than they expected. Over the course of our long friendship, she gave me more than I could ever return; and I was grateful. I learned to voice my feelings when I didn't want to do it her way.

Pam would have loved the Arlington Wetlands. Finding this place, wishing I could share its simple beauty with her, I really missed her. Especially now.

Chapter Nineteen

AUTUMN IN THE FIELD

Walking Ribbons in the Arlington Wetlands field was therapeutic, not only for the physical exercise, but because walking outdoors actually changed my mental perspective. This new adventure became a welcome escape.

At first I had walked briskly, looking around but not really seeing; I was still numb from loss. For a long time after Bob's death, it felt like I'd hit life's pause button. Everything seemed to have stalled inside me except the emotional pain. Life went on around me, but I was lost in my grief. I couldn't find a way out. I had assumed I'd get over this loss and soon return to normal; I didn't expect the sadness to last so long.

As I spent more time in the field, I began to really appreciate the simple beauty of this place. Walking gave me time to think about many things, and my thoughts began to rise freely from deep emotional places—about God, about Bob, and about my own life. The colorful flowers were cheerful, and the quiet peace was comforting. My thoughts gathered into descriptive phrases, but words were forgotten by the time I got home. So I stuck a little notebook and a pen in my pocket, and I recorded what I was thinking as Ribbons and I walked. My mind came alive out there in the open field, and words often flowed more freely than they did as I sat at my computer.

The morning hours in my office, while struggling for the right words, were periods of intense concentration. Out in that open field, the tension drained out of me; and the peace of nature settled over me like a warm, comforting shawl. As I walked among the beautiful flowers, the pain and sadness of grief slowly dissolved into the atmosphere.

What had begun as a simple task of walking the dog had now become a pilgrimage—a spiritual quest for understanding and healing. I was learning that the final stage of grief (the one labeled acceptance) might be further away than expected. So I kept walking in this place of solitude that God had provided.

It was fall, and the leaves were turning color. Autumn had always been my favorite season; and as I walked in the Wetlands field, poignant memories filled my emptiness.

My best autumn memories were of my experiences when participating in competitive trail rides with my first horse, Fanny. Pam had helped me with her training, and the joy of accomplishment and my newfound confidence had helped me cope with my unhappy marriage. I became obsessed with the exciting challenge of distance riding. I felt a thrill as we moved along at a fast trot through woods and fields, covering twenty-five miles of marked trail in a given time, usually about four hours. Fanny's strong competitive spirit carried me along, and her strength became a part of me. I savored the unique smell of fall and the sound of hooves crunching the dry leaves that covered the trails.

That same year that Pam had helped me train Fanny, I moved into an apartment; and I was separated from my husband for six months. That September, Pam invited me to go with her on an all-day hike with several friends. We started very early in the morning, and we walked through beautiful woods surrounding a large lake. While standing among those trees, my emotions brought me close to tears. I had a sense of deep longing—of missing something—and I remembered the wooded pasture of our farm while growing up. Why did the surrounding trees have such an effect on me? It was like coming home after a long absence.

We stopped to rest high on a hill, and we watched birds circling below us. When we came to an observation tower, a fleeting inspiration of courage led me to climb to the top in spite of my fear of heights. That day in the woods was the first time since childhood that I had so freely enjoyed nature's pleasures.

Later that fall, one autumn leaf became a symbol of God's grace. Overwhelmed with discouragement as I walked a city sidewalk one day on an errand from work, I suddenly noticed one colorful leaf directly in my path. It was the only leaf in sight that wasn't brown and dry and dead. I took it home, and it stayed fresh and bright for much longer than a leaf normally would. I treasured that leaf as a gift from God—to give me hope and to remind me of His enduring care for me.

My memories of fall rides, of pretty leaves, of hikes in the woods, and of times with Pam were still fresh in my mind. I still saved pretty autumn leaves. I picked them up as Ribbons and I walked to the field, and I took them home and put them in a box. Maybe I hold onto too many things; perhaps the losses of my past have created that need within me. I love the fragile beauty of nature. I love the colored leaves as pieces of my favorite season—a nostalgic time that ends too soon. I love the beauty of snow-covered tree branches and the graceful designs of snow drifts like those we had in Iowa, but winter's cold days are better enjoyed from inside a warm home. I certainly don't miss Iowa's winters.

In October one day, I saw that someone had placed a bench beside the pathway near the pond. I sat down on that hard bench, and I cried. I stared in front of me at the pond circled with brown grasses. I sat on that bench quite often during later walks, to let the peaceful scene quiet my spirit while listening to the songs of various birds in nearby trees. Ribbons would patiently wait, or she would sniff around the area nearby. A good girl in so many ways, she never went too far away even while off the leash.

When I heard a cardinal's cheery song, I wondered if it was the same bird that had awakened me several months earlier. A woodpecker's call reminded me of that same call I'd heard while walking the wooded pasture in Iowa. I often heard a bird I didn't recognize, and I was elated to find a phone app that helped me identify new birds.

Ribbons seemed to enjoy our walks as much as I did. As we strolled the pathway, grasshoppers would scatter from under our feet in unbelievable numbers, their wings making buzzy rattling sounds. She acted like she'd never seen grasshoppers before. Sometimes she would stop to watch the big black bugs that scooted across the path, totally oblivious that I had continued on. Not hearing a jingle of collar tags, I would stop and wait. When I called her, she would run to catch up.

One day Ribbons was more eager than usual, and she went ahead of me as we neared the pond. She stopped at a triangle of high grass, formed by the mowed trail around the pond meeting the trail from the entrance. I had often walked Ribbons around the triangle instead of just turning around to go home. I watched her as she stood for a moment on the path, peering into the higher grass. And then she ran into it. I saw her come out on the path near the pond, and then she ran at top speed around the triangle past me, and around again. I laughed out loud, and she stopped and looked at me—then ran around the triangle once more. I was still laughing as she came and jumped up on my knee, an exuberant doggie enjoying her freedom. She didn't act timid anymore, but such eager energy was rare.

Was she running that day for the sheer fun of it? Was she enjoying her freedom being off the leash? Was she more at ease with her new home?

Previously under very different circumstances, Ribbons had proved she could run fast. I remembered it as the day I learned not to yell at a timid dog. She had sniffed at something out in the grassy field one of the first times she was off the leash. I had yelled at her, "No!" and then I called her to "Come!"

Suddenly she was a black streak skimming across the field away from me, hardly touching the ground as she ran for home. Not once did she look back. She crossed the road and a parking area, and then she went out of sight around a mobile home. I knew she had to cross the road in front of our house, and I listened for the screech of brakes. All was quiet, and I was greatly relieved. When I got home, she was waiting in the yard. Without a word, I opened the front door; and she ran in and dived under the coffee table. At least she knew where home was, and she made it safely. I couldn't help but smile, remembering the black streak that seemed to skim over the grass toward home.

A sign near each entrance to the field explained the rules for dogs in the Wetlands. They must be on a leash, and owners must clean up after them. Since Ribbons was doing her business in the yard before our walks, I didn't have to worry about the second rule. I would keep her on the leash until I got within the privacy of the field, and then I would turn her loose. I once met a man on the trail with his dog also off the leash, and we smiled at each other and agreed that dogs needed freedom now and then.

As the weather cooled, I walked later in the day. With the sun above, everything was brighter, and the stillness of the pond mirrored skies of blue and wispy clouds of white. Tender green grass lined the water's edge, surrounded by a billow of taller grass with stems of tan, green, and purple, their delicate seed heads sprayed in graceful curved lines. Although I often took photos, they rarely captured the full beauty of what I saw.

Just as the field had a purpose within the wetlands environment, it had a purpose in my own life as it nourished my human need for comfort and peace. I didn't feel alone out there in that secluded, open area; I felt closer to God. His presence surrounded me and sheltered me from the outside world of pain. This was my healing place—where God made Himself known in a simple setting of His own creation. Each flower's beauty and fragrance, each birdsong, and each fluffy white cloud in the blue sky above spoke to me of His Sovereign wisdom and care.

Chapter Twenty

LINGERING TEARS

uring winter's cold months, I postponed my walks in the field until spring. And then it was February 24, 2014, twelve months after Bob's passing. I should be better by now—but I wasn't. I had honestly believed I would soon "get over" my grief, and life would get back to normal. I also thought my wrist should be healed from its injury by now so I could once again enjoy horseback riding.

A horse's hooves should be cleaned out often; but whenever I picked up Lady's foot, I couldn't hold it. The pain in my left wrist made me balance the foot on my knee instead. Cleaning four hooves took all my energy and patience. When I tried to lift the saddle onto her back, the pain often interfered with getting it in the right place. I didn't ride very often.

Riding Lady had been a pleasant diversion from grief after Bob died; I often wished I could keep riding! But everything I tried to do was physically painful, or it took more energy than I had. Sometimes I sat and stared into space, feeling too tired to move. I began to worry that my health was going bad. Was it my heart? When I shared my worry with a friend, she gently suggested, "Perhaps it is broken." I wondered how long it would take to mend.

It was probably depression, I decided—a normal stage of grief. I told myself to just keep going; it's supposed to get better.

Our trials should help us be more sensitive to the trials of others around us. Perhaps later, when our grief has lessened. At this point, I was sensitive only to reminders of Bob. I tried to cry in private, because I knew my tears made my husband sad, but tears often came without warning. A TV ad showed a young boy who reminded me of Bob when he was that age, and I cried. At church one morning, the organist played Bob's favorite hymn, and tears rolled down my cheeks. "Turn Your Eyes upon Jesus" was also one of my own favorites. I cried off and on most of that day.

Since high school, I had enjoyed singing in the choir but now my sensitivity often caused me to be overcome by emotion. One morning, while singing in the choir in front of the whole church, I began to cry. The woman next to me put her arm around me. Why does a simple act of caring cause tears to flow even more?

One day while straightening my desk now piled high by unfinished work, I saw a piece of paper with words scribbled in my own handwriting. I gasped as I recognized the message I had written to accompany the flowers I'd sent to Bob a week before he died: "Aloha, my son, with all my love. May God's angels guide you on your journey home." Reading those words triggered a sudden gushing of tears. But as I sat there at my desk sobbing uncontrollably, I suddenly felt God's presence like a hand on my shoulder. I sensed words: "It's alright now. It's over. He's okay. You're okay." I took a deep breath, and I was able to stop crying. It was a moment of incredible relief and reassurance.

The sadness remained, however, and I was still tired much of the time. My passion to ride a horse had been squelched by an injured tendon. My joy of living had been crushed by a broken heart. I sat, because it was difficult to do anything else. I could say I was fine, but I wasn't. I seemed to be disconnected from life, even from God.

Another morning, as I sat down to work at my computer, I noticed my devotional booklet on my desk. Not now, I told myself. I had other things to do. I suddenly realized that I was avoiding intimate time with God! Why? Was I avoiding Him because I blamed Him for my loss? Was I mad at Him?

In spite of my strong disappointment that Bob wasn't healed, I hadn't been aware of feelings of anger. I remembered hearing that depression and anger are related, and depression is anger turned inward. Was I angry at myself for not finding Bob's cure? Was I angry at God for not helping me find the cure? Was I hiding my resentment inside because I was afraid to admit feeling angry at God? I tried to be entirely honest as I considered my feelings. In a moment of insight, it was clear: I had gone to my room to pout, and I had shut the door on fellowship with the God who had disappointed me! I had broken our connection.

One day I heard a sermon that discussed adversity as a test of faith. The pastor explained how important our response was to difficult times. We can trust God to help us find understanding, or we can turn and walk away. We have a choice. I did not want to walk away from a God who had done so much to comfort me and to help me through these past few years. Even in the midst of my grief, I had much to be thankful for.

Influenced by this new perception, I knew I needed to truly forgive God for not healing Bob—not because God needed to be forgiven, certainly, but because I needed to reopen the door that I'd shut. I couldn't let whatever it was—whether disappointment, resentment, or anger—keep the door closed to intimate fellowship with my Lord! My relationship with Him was more important than anything else!

Grandpa Moats had often said: "God has always taken care of us. We'll take the bad with the good." Perhaps I had not fully understood the meaning behind his words before. I had always been happy to enjoy the good things in life; I just didn't want the bad stuff. I wanted all of life to be good stuff. But life is full of ups and downs; it isn't all pain or all joy. Each person's life is a unique tapestry woven of both. I'm finally beginning to understand how each and every experience has a purpose.

The painful times polish and refine the rough edges of my human character, while moments of joy encourage me to keep going. God never promised to protect me from all pain and sorrow, but He did promise to be with me whatever happens and to give me strength to endure it.

Someday the pain will be forever gone, but for now I must accept what God allows. He has given me so many wonderful blessings, and He has helped me through so many struggles; I should be willing to accept some losses.

He could have healed Bob, but He didn't. He must have had a reason. He asks me to have faith and trust His will even when I don't like it or don't understand. He doesn't have to explain His plan; God is Sovereign. I can choose each day whether to live my life as I want to, or to accept God's purpose. How does mortal man learn to accept God's will when it hurts this much?

If I acknowledge that God's will is best, and He is Sovereign over my life—and if I believe He has a good purpose for my life—then I would be wise to seek His guidance to stay on the path He has planned for me. I can say those words in my head, but my heart struggles with the pain—and the desire for relief.

My sorrow did not magically disappear just because of Scripture study, or prayer, or some insightful experience. Seeking God's help, however, through prayer and meditation on His Word was the only way to overcome such emotions. I had to depend on Him; I had to believe in His strength. I had to fill my mind with God's words of comfort, hope, and strength to prevent my own words from creeping in with negative consequences.

What was God trying to teach me? I considered the answer to that question, and I tried to apply it to my life at this point. I tried to see myself walking with God, studying His word, and allowing Him to work in my life.

On a Facebook group of Christian horse lovers, I found posted excerpts from a book titled *Morning Meditations from Your Abba Father*. The author, Alyse Best Muldoon, had lost both her husband and her father-in-law to cancer within a few days of each other. I had to get her book. As I read the daily meditations, I was touched by the words of love and comfort that God had shared with this woman. In each day's message, God reminded me that "I am with you. I am here beside you now." I realized once again how much His presence meant to me.

One day's message included this sentence: "Walk with Me to the other side of your grief." For many years, I had longed to feel I was walking with God. And here I was, walking a dog through a nearby field, believing that God had led me here. I thought of all the ways God had helped me in life and all the times He had spoken to me in one way or another. I suddenly realized that He had been walking beside me all along, even when I didn't feel His presence.

An image of the field's mowed pathway came to mind, and in that moment I saw it as my path to acceptance—the last stage of the grief process. Acceptance of death and loss. Acceptance of God's will to take Bob from this earth. Acceptance of peace.

Kim texted me one day: "God is very aware of our situation at every point in our life. May we be very aware of His presence." That was what I sincerely wanted! I wanted to feel His presence and know that He was with me. I wanted to feel that His Spirit was enabling me. An awareness of His presence pushes aside my anxiety and fear, at least for the moment. But I was still struggling to simply trust He was with me. Trust is the essence of faith.

Even when my faith was shaky, God had given me strength. God had not healed Bob of cancer, but He had given me a song of praise and words of assurance. He had sent a cardinal to awaken me to His Spirit's message. He had given us a dog to help me smile in spite of my worries, and then He gave us another dog that led me to a field where nature's beauty ministered to my sadness.

God had provided frequent reminders that He was with me in

spite of my doubts and questions, even during my depression and anger. God was still working with me, revealing His comforting love and His Sovereign wisdom. How could any child of God not see His Father's care in this picture? Perhaps we need to ask ourselves: do I really take time to look at what He is doing in my life? Can I learn to look beyond my present struggle, trusting God's promise to work it out according to His will?

Chapter Twenty-One

A NEW WILDERNESS

*T*he spring of 2014 was a season of reawakening for the field that had previously been agricultural land. Instead of crops, small trees and flowering shrubs were being planted among the grass and weeds. As a major part of the Arlington Wetlands project, the field was now open to the public. Interested groups or individuals could walk on mowed pathways through its emerging natural beauty to learn about its animals, birds, and flowers. Being so close to home, the Wetlands field became the place where I experienced my own season of renewal.

One morning, I noticed eight yellow metal posts placed at intervals around the field, and I assumed new signs were coming. To my surprise, a wooden bluebird nest box soon topped each post. Occupants arrived quickly; on my next visit I counted a dozen bluebirds. I couldn't wait to take photos of the new residents.

Two weeks later, the bluebirds were gone. Eastern Kingbirds were now sitting on the birdhouses and flying around the field, and I hadn't taken any pictures of the bluebirds. I assumed I would have more time.

When will I learn—life's opportunities don't wait for my convenience, and plans don't always work out as intended! The nest boxes were made for sweet bluebirds of happiness, not for those bold sassy kingbirds. I saw kingbirds quite often, but the bluebirds were a rare blessing. Why did I procrastinate?

Why does life rush by, with so many disappointments? I thought about three precious little boys named Mark, Bob, and David— and one was now gone, and my family would never be the same. I thought I would have more time with all of them.

Did God bring me to this field only to help me find peace and healing? Or was there something more? I began to wonder what lessons He had in store for me here. Perhaps to show me the fleeting nature of each moment so I would cherish life in a new way?

Chapter four of Matthew describes the testing of Jesus in the wilderness. Perhaps this field is my wilderness, and Bob's death is the testing of my faith. Losing a son had traumatized my Christian convictions. Could I overcome my disappointment? Would I emerge from here with a stronger faith?

The first time I had taken Ribbons to the park's grassy area to help her relieve herself, it was dawn. I remembered cumulus clouds filling the eastern sky, with bright rays of light shining down from between pieces of cloud like fingers reaching down from Heaven. "Crepuscular rays" they are called, according to a TV weatherman. It seems a strange name for such Heavenly glory!

I longed for more of those magical sunrise moments. So one morning very early, we walked into the newly discovered Wetlands field. As we neared the pond, something caught my eye; and I stopped to stare in awe. The rising sun's beams of light were spilling through the trees onto the water's surface, and I was reminded of sunlight streaming through colored glass windows in a church. There was a Holy reverence over the scene before me, and for a moment I felt I was standing in the very presence of the Creator Himself. I thought of Psalm 46:10 (NIV): "Be still, and know that I am God."

CREPUSCULAR RAYS OVER THE GRASSY AREA

As the sun made its way upward, I watched the piercing light rays and changing shadows move slowly with a sense of quiet purpose. I saw the promise of a new day in that sunrise as a gift—a message of hope from God. Today's world seems to have so little hope. Perhaps we need to take time to appreciate a morning sunrise as a reminder of God's sovereign power and purpose.

On my office wall is a framed saying from a past church bulletin: "Every morning, lean thine arm awhile upon the windowsill of Heaven to gaze upon thy God. Then, with the vision in thine heart, turn, strong, to meet the day." I am thankful to the unknown writer of that piece of inspiration. I know I need God's strength for the day ahead; my own is never enough. When I take the time each morning to seek a vision of who He is, it is easier to trust His protection and guidance throughout the day.

That morning near the pond, I saw such a vision. I could imagine Him as a Holy Sovereign God—a God of love and goodness—and a powerful Creator of the universe. Such a vision can change our lives. Too often our struggles dim our vision of who He really is. Too often we neglect to take the time to sit in His presence and let His spirit reveal Himself to us. Usually, we are too busy trying to live our lives without Him.

Beyond the inspiration of sunrise over the Wetlands, I also enjoyed the variety of wildflowers in the field. Photos on one of two large signs near the boardwalk depicted the Prairie Coreopsis, a flower I'd never seen, and a cactus.

In May, plain yellow Coreopsis dotted the landscape—a flower I knew because I had bought some from Walmart for my own garden. How, I wondered, did they get into this field? In June, I finally saw the Prairie Coreopsis pictured on the sign as it began to blossom in clusters around the pond. The two species looked alike except for the red centers in the Prairie variety.

Walking past the pond one day, I saw red flowers. Four sprigs of blooms looked just like the Prairie Coreopsis, but their petals were red, not yellow. Searching online, I found a description of the Prairie Coreopsis as "bright yellow with mahogany red centers, rarely pure dark red." Wow! I knew I'd discovered something rare (and of course I took photos). Had anyone else seen those red flowers? Did they know they were unusual? To me, those red Prairie Coreopsis flowers were a special blessing from God. But this whole field was a blessing!

The Arlington Wetlands area became for me a study of nature. That year, I watched the landscape change from day to day, season to season, as new life in spring succumbed to the heat of summer, and then autumn's changing colors blew away leaving naked trees in winter's cold. Within those scenes of changing seasons and weather, and the varying moods of morning, daytime, and evening, I realized how my own moods changed. Warm sunny days drew me into the field; colder dreary days were better enjoyed at home.

A few years earlier, I had seen how a lack of rain drained the swampy wetlands lake until the swan parents left. After we had plenty of rain, the water rose back to its former level. I realized how much the weather influences all of life.

My folks had depended on the weather for good crops to feed us and our animals, knowing that all the hard work that went into farming could be wasted by a season of drought or a strong storm. One hot summer day, when I was raking hay with our team of Percherons, I'd had a flash of epiphany. I had stopped to rest them in the shade at the edge of the field. I smelled their sweat, and I heard their heavy breathing and the creaking of the harness as they moved to swish away the flies. I wiped away my own sweat as I watched a hawk circling slowly in the distance, in the valley below us.

At that moment, I sensed an awareness of connection and of belonging to this land—not from a liturgy of dust returning to dust, but from a reverent consideration of the Creator of this Earth who gave us the rain and the sun to help our crops grow. I was a farmer at heart. We depended on God for all we had, and He took care of us. I realized at that moment why my folks were thankful for what we had, even though it didn't seem like much. We trusted God for our future.

Chapter Twenty-Two

CLOUDS OF GLORY

Nature itself often influenced my thoughts as I walked the field with Ribbons. As I neared the pond one summer day, the sky became dark, and I wondered if I should quickly head for home. I'm glad I didn't.

There was a sudden rush of wind and a loud rustling of leaves in the nearby trees. A stout gusty force pushed me back, and I had to brace myself against it. Ribbons stood quietly facing me, her fur blown up around her neck. A layer of low heavy thick clouds moved rapidly toward us, their dark shadows approaching menacingly over the field like creeping ooze. Far above, a higher level of thin white clouds remained still, as though silently watching. It was strange to see two levels of clouds so different in mood and movement. I watched with fascination as the shadows came closer, and the heavy dark clouds swept over us so close above me that it seemed I could almost touch them. Ribbons and I were suddenly immersed into a mysterious darkness.

As quickly as they had come, the heavy gray clouds moved on into the distance beyond the trees. Night turned back into day, and the sky was blue again. Only the wispy white clouds remained high above. I had seen no rain, no storm, and no lightning—just heavy clouds passing quickly overhead as if driven by some unseen urgency. I stood there in awe of nature's declaration of its own energy.

Words of Scripture came to mind from Psalm 19:1 (NIV): "The Heavens declare the glory of God; the skies proclaim the work of His hands." It was as though I had seen a glimpse of His power and majesty in those fast moving dark clouds.

Once before, I had seen His magnificent glory in the clouds—the day before my tonsillectomy when I was seventeen. I had missed two weeks of school every winter because of tonsillitis and pneumonia, and Doc Grant had often suggested having my tonsils taken out. Money was scarce, so Dad had put it off until the summer before I left for college. Although it was a simple procedure, I was quite anxious about my first operation.

We were harvesting oats that day on our Iowa farm; and between loads, I sat on the ground against a shock of oats as I looked up at the clouds. The August sky was a bold blue background for a magnificent display of deep layers of white cottony billows. I could see giant pillars and domes within those incredible formations, and I imagined a distant city of white—like Heaven itself. I was totally captivated by the scene above me, and I wondered if God could have arranged those clouds just for me. I decided that if He could create such majestic splendor in the sky, He could surely take care of me during a simple operation. That glimpse of Heavenly glory became a memorable milestone in my Christian experience.

On an August day in an Iowa field, God had helped me face my first surgery. Here in this Arlington Wetlands field in Illinois, God had once again sent clouds to display His glory; and I knew He was now helping me through the loss of my son. I believe we find our strength from trusting in His. Faith itself has mysterious power.

Chapter Twenty-Three

SURRENDER

*D*uring my high school and college years, I had often sensed God asking me to surrender my life to Him. I wanted to be a real Christian, but I didn't want to be a missionary in Africa. God hadn't asked that of me, but I was afraid He would. I had read Scripture passages about the persecution and killing of Christians. Those images haunted me. I wasn't ready for such commitment and sacrifice, and I was afraid to even take the first step.

Total surrender sounded so extreme. I believed in God; wasn't that enough? I was raised in church. I was told to do my best, and God would understand. I had read my Bible, and I knew that Jesus told Nicodemus in John 3:7 (NIV) that "...you must be born again." No one had explained what those words meant.

It took the death of my grandfather to jolt me into a serious spiritual quest. I was twenty-six then, I was married with three sons under four years of age, and I had no knowledge yet of the problems between my mother and my grandfather. Grandpa Moats had always been my beloved "Dompa." In his mellow-aged voice, he had often sung me to sleep with "Preacher and the Bear," or "There's a Long,

Long Trail A-winding." I'm sure I was the only toddler in the world who begged for those particular bedtime songs!

Grandpa's stories about his horses fascinated me. He had been a blacksmith before he married Grandma and started farming; she had taught in a one-room schoolhouse before becoming a farmer's wife. Grandpa always had a team of work animals as long as he was on the farm. When I was a toddler he had mules named Jack and Jim, and sometimes he let me lead them to the water tank after a day's work in the field. We moved from Iowa to Montana where he had a team of Belgians, and we returned to Iowa three years later when I was eight years old. He then bought a team of Percheron mares, Bell and Doll, and Bell became my first riding horse. Through my contact with Grandpa's horses and from hearing stories about all the horses he had owned and trained, I found a growing passion within me to someday have my own horse.

Grandpa's death was difficult to accept. I was there when he died, six days after his stroke. For the first time, I saw how quickly life leaves the body when the time comes—silently disappearing into another dimension. With a wiser reverence for the Almighty, who holds all life in His hands, I decided to think more carefully about putting off my response to His will.

My early beliefs came from my folks. But each of us must find our own understanding, our own personal relationship with Deity, and our own assurance.

Bob was three years old when Pastor Roy Gibbs and his wife Dora knocked on our door to invite us to their new church. I felt uneasy when his sermons mentioned surrender, but he personally answered my searching questions with sensitive wisdom. I began to sincerely crave the love of God that I saw in that small Wesleyan congregation.

During the Christmas season, while others were merrily celebrating the birth of Jesus, I was praying desperately to receive Him into my heart. I asked God to "save" me by Easter; I hoped three months would give Him enough time.

A few weeks later on a Sunday morning in January of 1967, it happened during the closing prayer. Random pieces of the spiritual puzzle all suddenly fell in place— words of that closing prayer, of many sermons, hymns and Scripture readings—and I suddenly understood the life-changing message Pastor Gibbs had been preaching. I had always thought I was a Christian because I was raised in a Christian family and believed in God. I knew that Jesus had died on a cross for the sins of the world. But that morning, my faith became personal. I realized He had died on that cross for me and for my sin. As I considered my unworthiness, I sensed His whisper, "I've already taken care of it."

In that moment, I was incredibly aware of His love and forgiveness, and I felt a profound sense of peace and joy. I believed I had been given the opportunity to start over with a new life. From a positive knowing came the words, "I am His, and He is mine!" It was the beginning of a genuine, intimate relationship with Jesus, the Son of God—my Savior. Pastor Gibbs had explained what it meant to be "born again," and I had actually experienced it!

When I gave my life to Jesus that morning, I had no way of knowing that my surrender would one day be tested by the loss of a son. By then I had already learned that true surrender extends beyond one emotional decision. Each morning is a new opportunity to renew the vow, and each day's struggles test my commitment.

Bob's death was the test that shook the foundation of my faith. Years earlier, many people had prayed for my son David and he was healed through a liver transplant. This time we had prayed for Bob, and God had given no healing. In Matthew 21:22 (NIV), Jesus told His disciples: "If you believe, you will receive whatever you ask for in prayer." But I thought I did believe—until my grief led to the doubts and questions that overwhelmed me! Was my faith not strong enough? Was Scripture wrong? Did I still belong in God's family?

I had asked God that question before. While on my way to visit my friend Pam, many years earlier, I had prayed for assurance as I drove. "Lord, am I still yours?" The radio was on, and when the very next song began I immediately knew God's answer. My eyes filled with tears as I listened to all the words until the chorus ended, "I am His, and He is mine." The words of that familiar hymn again filled my heart with thankful joy.

Maintaining a daily intimate fellowship with God is an important part of a genuine Christian life—but things happen. The aftermath of Bob's death had interrupted that relationship in my life. I never stopped going to church, and I never stopped praying. I still believed in God, but my efforts were limited. I had questions, but I no longer studied His Word to find answers. Walking in the Wetlands field was my escape and my comfort as I enjoyed the peace and beauty of nature. I was thankful for God's presence there, but I struggled with anything more.

Facing the issue of mortality—my own mortality—was causing a growing fear of death. Sooner or later, we all die. Bob died. I will die. I believed in Heaven, and God's words of assurance before Bob's death were a definite assurance. So why had I become so preoccupied with this issue? Perhaps I hadn't taken it so personally until now. I was seventy-three, and Russ was eighty-three when Bob died. One never knows how many years are left.

One day I realized I was afraid of losing my husband. If something would happen to him, I was afraid I couldn't handle it. I didn't want to go anywhere without him. I didn't want to be alone. If something did happen, would I be able to take care of him? What if something happened to me, and I couldn't take care of him? I wanted to trust that God would be with me whatever happened, but I found myself thinking negative thoughts. That only made it worse, but I couldn't stop worrying.

I did not like getting old and facing the end of things as I knew them. I had many plans. Would I have time to finish them? I also didn't want to leave a cluttered home full of possessions for someone else to deal with. Thinking about all my stuff someday being tossed into a dumpster made me cry. I remembered the auctions after my dad passed away and after my first husband died.

It wasn't valuable "stuff," but much of it had meaning because of a connection to a family member. Russ reminded me that it wouldn't matter after I was gone. How wise of him, this man who accumulated very little "stuff."

The cardinal's persistent visits many months ago had inspired me to go back to mornings alone with God. After we got Ribbons, I had become totally involved with her training. I saw how my "focus" had shifted.

Experience with horses had taught me about focus. A rider's focus gives direction to the horse. If my mind dwells on a fearful object ahead, my horse will likely become nervous. But if I calmly focus on something safe beyond that object, my horse will often walk on by. If I worry about a problem, that problem becomes my main focus. If I meditate on God's Word, He draws me closer—and I can focus on His presence in my life. My focus on God is my connection to His guidance.

We can easily lose focus and become distracted by losses, by circumstances, and countless human issues. While mourning the loss of my son, my attention moved away from a thankful trust in God's all-sufficient provision. I felt overwhelmed and afraid. In spite of God's many blessings, I'd lost focus on God as the unseen Source of my hope and strength.

Many years ago, I had an experience that taught me a valuable lesson on focus, and I shared that experience with Bob before he died. Forty miles southwest of Colorado Springs, the Royal Gorge Bridge is the highest suspension bridge in the world, spanning a narrow rocky gorge 1,053 feet deep. I walked on that bridge one day when it happened to be closed to vehicles—a coincidence that probably wasn't one.

Reaching a spot halfway across the bridge, I realized it was swaying in the wind currents moving through the gorge. Looking down, I could see the Arkansas River at the bottom of the chasm, like a glistening narrow silver ribbon beside a miniature railway. I had always been afraid of heights. In a state of panic, I imagined the worst.

Looking around made me dizzy. But many people were walking beside me with no sign of fear, so I convinced myself to keep going. I kept my eyes fixed on the opposite end of the bridge, where souvenir shops waited. Walking back was easier.

The next day, a conference speaker used Hebrews 12:1-3 (NIV) for the basis of his message as he told of Paul's admonition to keep our eyes fixed "on Jesus, the author and perfecter of our faith" so we will not lose courage. The Phillips translation of the same passage refers to Jesus as "the source and the goal of our faith." In my mind I could see the Royal Gorge Bridge as I walked its 1,260 foot length one step at a time—as I looked toward the other end, the goal, instead of down at possible danger below. It was a perfect illustration of God's Word!

As I walked the path of the Arlington Wetlands field, I remembered that I had decided to go through life the same way—one day at a time, one step at a time, focusing on Christ as the image of my goal. He is the unseen Source of my courage and strength.

I first believed that God led me into the Wetlands field to deal with my loss. But I could see now that He was helping me refocus on my relationship with Him. God's presence within that field had been very real. Beyond my enjoyment of the field and its flowers, more than the inspiration and peace of nature's surroundings, this pilgrimage was drawing me closer to the Creator Himself.

THE JOY OF HIS PRESENCE

"You have made known to me the path of life; You will fill me with joy in Your presence, with eternal pleasures at Your right hand." Psalm 16:11 (NIV)

*O*n an early fall morning in 2014, I stood on the path near the pond as I watched the sun move up from behind the trees. It emerged suddenly, splashing a wash of rich color over everything around me.

Months earlier, yellow flowers and fern-like green leaves had come from each green Partridge Pea stem. Now the same stems were brown, adorned only with dry curled leaves and reddish seed pods; but their color was more intense in the sunlight. Tan-colored grasses at the pond's edge shimmered, their gracefully arched stems glistening with dewy wetness. I no longer looked without seeing. Nature's simple beauty was clearly a work of God's creation.

Hesitant to leave, I stood still. This field had become my "Holy Ground." Even as the sun slid under a cloud, the sacredness of the moment remained like the essence of God's presence. How often do we stand within a bubble of God's grace, enclosed by His unconditional love? How often do we wait in the light of His Holy presence? Is it all the time—and we are not aware of it? Have I been standing in his grace my whole life?

Awareness is a gift, perhaps, or an assurance we learn through experience. There is great joy in knowing that I am His, and He is mine. Here in this field, I have felt a distinctive awareness of His presence—not as some distant judge or critical authority—but as an enabling Spirit actively working in and through me toward a more intimate fellowship. God waits for me here, for my worship and for my communion with Him.

I can't see God, but I can see His creation. I see evidence of His wisdom and His love of beauty in each flower, in each bird, in the wind, the clouds, and the sky. Scripture says that God created man with a need for a relationship with his Creator. I've often sensed that need. My relationship with Him is my source of strength and peace. My dependence on Him lifts me above my human limitations and earthly problems—not to escape them, but to find the power through His Spirit to deal with them.

God says to be strong and of good courage. I can only know such strength and courage by depending on Him. Scripture says He has promised to always be with me, so I need to believe it. Without trust, there is fear and uncertainty. I know those two emotions all too well.

One of my favorite verses is Colossians 1:27 in the Phillips translation: "And the secret is simply this: Christ in you! Yes, Christ in you bringing with Him the hope of all the glorious things to come." We know that Christ lives in us as we experience a real relationship. It's the communication of God to man and the prayers of man to God. It's the reverence we feel toward Almighty God, and the submission of our wills to His. Do I believe it with all my heart? Do I really trust that He is in control? That He has a purpose? My struggles through difficult times have often taught me the most about believing.

As I sat on the bench by the pond, His love surrounded me. Even when tears of sadness rolled down my cheeks, I sensed His Spirit's presence in a gentle breeze. The sun warmed my back. Birds sang their cheerful songs. This field was a safe, comforting place under a sheltering ceiling of sky and cloud. The nearby trees stood like a surrounding wall of protection. I looked upward into the open sky to the Creator of this place. I didn't feel alone here. It was easier, here, to think about Bob.

God's presence hadn't always seemed so real. In past times and places, I remember feeling lost and alone; and I was often overwhelmed by unanswered questions or difficult decisions. Knowing I should simply trust Him and wait for His guidance is the ideal, but that part of me is still a work in progress.

Perhaps the Wetlands field was God's gift of a special time and place for me to experience His loving, healing presence—where He could speak to me through His creation.

As I think of my daughter-in-law, I pray that her sadness of being alone may soon change to peace and joy. I think of my granddaughters who stood in front of hundreds of people to sing about the love that goes on and on after we say goodbye. I pray that God's love will be known by each one of us—an intimate, unconditional, compassionate love that comforts, strengthens, and provides the hope and assurance that we need. It is God's love that continues on and on, and that love is available to anyone at any time. We need only to seek Him and open our hearts and minds to receive His presence. We need only to shut out the world around us, and take time to be alone with Him.

His love is not the kind that gives in to our selfish wants; it is a love that draws us closer to Himself so we can follow His will for our lives. He sees each one of us in all our human weakness and need, and He loves us anyway. We must trust His wisdom. He knows the whole plan—past, present and future. He sees eternity.

Chapter Twenty-Five

REFOCUS; MOVE ON

I clearly remember the first time Russ and I rode our horses in the field behind the stable where I met him. "Look at this beautiful day that God has given us," he had said with a smile. He had noticed my depression. With his positive Irish outlook, he reminded me of God's blessings. He helped me to look beyond an unhappy marriage and the trauma of almost losing a son from liver failure.

My mind had become stuck on the ordeal of David's transplant. I see now that in order to move on from any stressful experience, we need to refocus on a new direction. I needed to stop reliving those fearful moments in the hospital, and be thankful that God had worked a life-giving miracle for David.

Since losing Bob, I had again become stuck on the stress of the experience itself as I relived the sadness again and again. My walks in the Arlington Wetlands led me in a new direction, and I found delight in nature's beauty. Those walks began as a very real physical journey with small but inspiring discoveries each day. Bright flowers in an open field cheered my hurting soul. Nature's serenity seeped into my spirit. Walking awakened my body. It was a slow process, to feel whole again after a long season of feeling shattered. It takes time to heal.

Meanwhile, it was also a metaphorical pilgrimage; it was an emotional journey of spiritual renewal while examining my beliefs and convictions. Within the natural setting of God's creation, the Creator himself drew me into His loving presence and encouraged me to refocus on Him instead of my loss.

As I considered this issue, three words came to mind: "center and grow." It was a phrase often used by Sally Swift, founder of Centered Riding principles. Because Ms. Swift and her basic principles had meant so much to my riding experiences, I had explained them quite thoroughly in my first book. At any transition, she would tell her students to center on one's energy within and grow tall and straight like a tree, not from forcing it but from allowing it. I had tried to apply that principle to my spiritual life as I tried to center on Christ my source of energy and grow from my experiences. Now, I needed to once again center on His presence and refocus on His Spirit at work instead of trying to do it myself.

While enjoying the field's natural beauty, I learned an important lesson. I noticed that each flower had its moment of glory. When one flower was gone, another took its place. After the plain Coreopsis bloomed its cheerful yellow in May, the Prairie Coreopsis came along in June with its own yellow petals and red centers. In July, I saw the sturdy golden blossoms of black-eyed Susans. And in August, the Partridge Pea returned with its spreading yellow fragrance. I realized that even the flowers followed the natural cycle of life and loss.

It was easy to accept the loss of a lovely flower; there were always more flowers. Accepting the loss of a child was not so easy. There had been only one Bob. I had expected to keep all three of my wonderful sons, but I was deeply thankful for the two I still had. Like the beauty of the flowers, nothing lasts forever. I told myself that the earthly pain of loss was also temporary.

When I had first entered the field in August of 2013, only a few stalks of Partridge Pea blossomed near the mowed pathway. Now, a year later, I saw a field of yellowness on both sides of the path. I walked between those fragrant flowers, hearing the buzz of countless bees as they swarmed among the inviting blossoms. Yellow was not my favorite color, but its cheery brightness had lifted my spirits.

Everything has its fleeting place in time, I realized—spring's renewal, the blue summer sky, the colorful autumn leaves, and the cold of winter. Life goes on. I had lost other loved ones and gotten through the sadness. Time heals all wounds, they say. Have "they" ever lost a child?

This loss was different. Perhaps because I was older now, it had forced me to confront my own mortality. It had challenged the depth of my relationship with God, and it had revealed flaws in my faith. As I searched for understanding, I happened one day to read the words: "Adversity is a revealer of our strengths and weaknesses." The loss of my son had made me especially aware of my fear of death. Would it also reveal the inner strength that I needed? Why was it so difficult to remember that "God is my strength?"

God had done so much for me! He had been faithful in spite of my inconsistency. Why did I so often feel uncertain and distant from His love? Did it have anything to do with my uncertain childhood without a mother? Or was it because of my inconsistency in reading God's Word and spending time in His presence?

Bob's daughters had sung: "Life is brief, but when it's gone, love goes on and on." Unlike the fleeting flowers and unlike our human lives on this earth, God's love has no end. When human life ends on earth and moves into a new dimension, God's love will continue on within eternity. And there I will finally know His love as it was meant to be known—a complete love always surrounding me to never again be questioned. Our hope of Heaven is meant to be encouraging. Heaven is what I look forward to as I maneuver through this earthly journey. My faith is based on that hope.

While walking the field, I was puzzled at the abundance of so many species of yellow flowers. Shouldn't there be more variety of color? I later talked to someone in charge of the field who told me that a mixture of seeds had been planted when the pond was dug. A lack of rain that year may have kept some of the seeds from germinating. Weather, then, had influenced the color of the field!

As I passed the pond one morning in August of 2014, something new caught my eye—one purplish-pink coneflower in bloom near the path. I thought it strange there was only one. On my next walk, I again saw the single coneflower, almost hidden behind the taller Partridge Peas—one new purple blossom, my favorite color, within all the yellowness!

A few days later, I couldn't find the coneflower. How could a flower vanish? I walked back and forth, searching, until I saw it laying dead on the ground, dry and lifeless, its roots without soil. How did that happen? I took it home, and I put it in a glass of water. It did not revive.

I mourned the short life of that one purple cone flower. I was frustrated that someone had pulled it out of the ground and robbed the world of its beauty. I had hoped to fix that flower, to bring it back to life. I had tried to fix Bob's cancer, too. My intentions were good, but I cannot solve every problem.

Human nature isn't perfect. I knew my relationship with God had great importance, but I often neglected it. I knew I wasn't spending enough time in serious prayer, meditation, and Bible study, but there were always so many other things that I needed to do. Was it just out of habit? Or was I still avoiding time with God on purpose—disappointed that God hadn't healed Bob? I had prayed for a miracle. I didn't get it. Was it my human selfish nature? It was difficult to admit; but if I wanted to change, I had to see what needed changing.

For some reason, I must keep reminding myself that God is my Father and I am His child. He is the Sovereign God of the Universe! I have no right to expect Him to do whatever I want. God has blessed me, and He has been with me through my loss. I am here to serve and worship Him, not the other way around.

Many years ago, when I was miserable and discouraged, I spent one to three hours a day alone with God. I felt a great need back then to seek His help. Now that I am happier, that desperate need is absent. Do we only seek God when we are in trouble? Do we forget our human need for daily fellowship, guidance, and strength when life is good?

As I considered my disappointment that God had not healed Bob, I discovered another word: disillusionment. Strange, how my heart suddenly understood that word so clearly as I recognized it within me. I was ashamed.

My faith was inconsistent because I lacked discipline. I wrote about God's love and greatness, and yet I often felt helpless. I experienced wondrous moments of His presence in the field, and yet I often felt alone. Riding instructors had also mentioned my inconsistent ways. I lived by my emotions. Don't we all do that? Isn't it just being human?

"Faith, not feelings," I'd been told so many times. I needed to develop my self-discipline. I knew that I needed God's help; I couldn't do it alone.

I was grateful that Russ understood me. He had lost one son before I knew him, and he'd lost another son two years after I lost Bob. I was glad we could talk honestly about our feelings and beliefs. Our discussions were precious. He could usually bring me out of my periods of sadness.

As one friend put it, it was time to shut the door on my tears and move on. It was time to stop feeling sorry for myself. When will I find the peace of acceptance, I wondered—the final stage of the grief process? I wanted my journey of grief to be over.

One day, a lovely butterfly lit on a flower beside the field's path, slowly opening and closing its delicate wings. Was it a Monarch? I stopped to watch. It flew on. I followed. I tried to memorize its distinctive pattern of orange and brown colors so I could later find it in my butterfly book. I pursued as it flitted from flower to flower until it flew off out of sight.

Perhaps my search for "acceptance" is like the pursuit of that butterfly. Acceptance is not the end of the journey after all; it is many moments that come and go as one's life begins to refocus on new beginnings. Its presence is a blessing to be treasured. You simply continue walking the path before you, encouraged and strengthened by the many blessings that God has given. You keep on going, step by step; and you deal with whatever you find in your path, trusting that God is with you and He will always take care of you. It works best when you truly believe it.

Chapter Twenty-Six

LEAVING THE HEALING FIELD

The winter of 2014 seemed unusually long. I could hardly wait to go back to the field. On a warm January afternoon, as I walked Ribbons in that direction, a nearby resident stopped me. He warned me that he and his wife had seen a pack of a dozen coyotes several times, running through the park's grassy area into the Wetlands field at dusk.

I already knew two coyotes had been seen boldly walking on the road through our park in the daytime, and perhaps it was the same two that had been seen going out onto our frozen lake after the ducks and geese. All of those birds had gradually disappeared.

Two coyotes didn't scare me. But little Ribbons and I might have trouble with a large pack of them in that secluded field. I decided to not take any chances. We did not enter the field for several months, while I talked to conservation police and people in charge of the field, hoping for something to be done.

I was so sure that God had led me into the Arlington Wetlands to heal my grief; why did the coyotes have to spoil everything? Why would God lead me to that healing place and then allow the coyotes to scare me away? Romans 8:28 (NIV) affirms that "in all things

God works for the good of those who love Him and who have been called according to His purpose." So what good were the coyotes? Did God have a reason to keep me out of the field?

That spring of 2015 brought even more disappointments. Ever since I'd sprained my wrist tendon in September of 2013, it still hurt to lift a saddle onto Lady's back. It was difficult to clean her stall. For more than a year, I hadn't been able to ride very much. Taking care of a horse drained my energy, and I felt old and tired. Over the winter I had paid the stable owner to take care of Lady, and I felt guilty for not being able to do it myself. I missed the relationship I'd always enjoyed with horses.

In November 2014, as I slid off a stack of hay bales, I had landed flat on my back. Fortunately, I checked out OK except for strained neck muscles. Then in December, I woke up at three a.m. one morning wondering if I was having a heart attack. I decided it was pleurisy. I'd had pleurisy pain now and then all my life, but this time it was more severe and lasted much longer than usual. Our doctor told me it wasn't pleurisy. It was "costochondritis," another name for chest wall pain, possibly a side effect of my fall. Treatment included a heating pad and pain pills, and it lasted a few months.

No longer able to enjoy my horse, I was totally disheartened by my physical problems. At seventy-six years old, after forty-one years of riding and owning horses, I began to wonder if that part of my life was over. I told a few friends who knew Lady that I would sell her to the right owner. I couldn't bring myself to actually list her for sale, however. I wanted God to show me what to do; if I was supposed to sell my last horse, I wanted Him to bring me the right buyer. I wasn't quite ready to let go.

February 24, 2015, marked the two-year anniversary of Bob's death. Easter—the season of self-examination and repentance—was only a few weeks away. Perhaps it was a good time for me to seriously look at my own life.

I knew I was a Christian, forgiven and adopted into God's family, but I didn't feel the same joy I once had. Past regrets and the guilt of past decisions had piled up inside me for too long, and I could no longer just push that pile aside. My disillusionment that Bob hadn't been healed was limiting my fellowship with God. The aftermath of loss had revealed flaws in my faith. And now my lifelong passion for riding seemed to be slipping away. I remembered how God had asked for my surrender when I was young and how I had put it off until after Grandpa Moats died. I realized that my stubborn resistance often made a wall between me and God. Perhaps it was time to deal with all of it.

It was time to tear down that wall!

Jesus had taken upon His innocent shoulders all the sin of the world because He loved each one of us that much, and it was the only way to pay the price of sin. He died in my place to take away my guilt. Do we ever fully understand such love and mercy?

I decided to give up my guilt for Lent.

Jesus died so that I could drown my sin in the waters of baptism and live a new life free of guilt. On the cross, He had said "It is finished." I remembered that He had once whispered to me that "I've already taken care of it."

Repentance involves a change of direction to follow a different path than before. I saw my disillusionment for the sin it was—a headstrong tendency to want my own way. I needed to renew my commitment of surrender. I needed to make an effort to seek God's presence outside of the field.

After all, it wasn't the field that gave healing, it was God's presence; and He could make Himself known anywhere. I had felt His guiding presence in a hospital room when He put it in my heart to pray for healing for David's liver failure. I had felt His healing presence in the office of a former employer when He sent a stranger to pray for my spinal problem and physically touch me with God's power. I had sensed His silent words of assurance as I lay in bed praying for Bob as he was dying. And then for almost two years, God had made his comforting presence known to me as I walked the paths in the nearby field.

Although I wanted Easter of 2015 to settle my spiritual situation once and for all, it was more like a computer restart. The leftover internal programming of my humanity was still struggling with yielding to God's will. I was aware, however, that the sun had risen on a new day. I turned to Philippians 3:13-14 (NIV): "But one thing I do: forgetting what is behind and straining toward what is ahead, I press on toward the goal to win the prize for which God has called me heavenward in Christ Jesus."

God had drawn me into the field, and He had made me more aware of His unconditional love and care. He had also showed me that I needed to protect and develop my intimate fellowship with His Spirit. I was determined to respond with a renewed commitment to spend time in His presence more consistently.

By the first of May that year, I had made a life-changing decision. My friend Mary Ann wanted to buy Lady, and I knew it would be a good home. It took me a few weeks to convince myself to actually go through with it, but I believed God had worked it out.

Giving up horses had previously been unimaginable. I'd had Lady for eleven years. I loved her. We'd had a strong bond in spite of her headstrong ways. I had enjoyed some great trail rides, several horse shows, and the challenge of one very special competitive ride that gave me that winning feeling even without an award. Lady had helped me learn the importance of confidence, and she had been the motivation for my second book. I'm thankful for that last summer with her after Bob died; it turned out to be a fitting closure to my lifelong passion with horses. Now it was time to let go.

I cried as I told her goodbye. I watched as Mary Ann loaded her into the trailer, but I didn't watch as they drove away. When I was asked to come take pictures of Lady in her new home, I put it off as long as I could. When I finally did go, I saw how attentive she was to her new owner while she totally ignored me. It hurt even more than I had imagined. But I knew it was best that way.

This was not an easy time for me. My horses were gone, and I knew I'd never own one again. It was the loss of a lifetime passion.

Bob was gone, and I didn't see the rest of my family much anymore. Lil was gone. Pam was gone. We still had Ribbons, but I hadn't walked in my healing field for months. Russ was my support and the love of my life. I clung to him more than ever.

In Job 1:21 (NIV), although Job had lost his children and all of his possessions, his faith enabled him to say "The Lord gave and the Lord has taken away; may the name of the Lord be praised." He did not harbor resentment against God because of his losses. And God later blessed him with more children and great wealth.

I had been taught that everything we have on this earth is given by God, and He has final control of it all. We are to hold our possessions in an open hand and be willing to let go of anything, including loved ones, when that is God's will.

Those words could be said more easily than sincerely accepted. I was still struggling with overwhelming disappointment—and perhaps a bit of resentment. For too many years, I had tried to fix the relationship with my first husband; and it had resulted in misery and failure. I had tried to fix Lady's headstrong nature, Lil's demanding ways, and Ribbons' timid personality. I had searched for a cure for Bob's disease. I wanted to bring a dead purple coneflower back to life. Did I think I had to solve every problem? Or was it my pride? Only God had the power, and yet I remember telling myself that not everyone is healed. Why couldn't I accept the things I couldn't change?

While reading an entry in *Jesus Calling,* a book by Sarah Young, I was reminded that God's favor doesn't totally depend on what I do. Focusing on performance becomes "a source of deep discouragement when your works don't measure up to your expectations." I understood that God was speaking those words directly to me! I realized I was trying to be in control of my world instead of depending on the guidance of an omnipotent God.

This was nothing new. One morning many years earlier during a summer church camp, I had told God I couldn't be the victorious Christian that everyone expected. Immediately I sensed His response: "Let ME do it through you!" I got out of bed and went to the chapel service, and I felt His presence more than ever. But again, my inconsistent feelings later took over. Why did this have to be such a struggle? Why couldn't I let Him do His will in me all of the time? Was it simply because I sometimes wanted my own way? Was my lack of surrender the problem?

Or was I simply being human?

In time, I remembered the words printed on a plaque on my wall: "I will lift up mine eyes unto the hills, from whence cometh my help." Those words were from Psalm 121:1 (KJV). Verse two continues: "My help cometh from the Lord, which made heaven and earth." The God who made this world and every living thing on it is the same God who helps each one of us each day of our lives.

Thankfully, there was a time when I had known His Spirit's help and guidance. His presence gave me joy and strength. When my negative emotions take over, however, they cloud the awareness of His presence. I have found I can lift that cloud with thanksgiving and praise—praise that He is an awesome God who understands our human nature and thanksgiving that He has provided for our needs.

That summer of 2015 was probably safe for me to walk in the field; but something always got in the way. It was too wet, or too cold, or too hot, or the wood ticks were bad, or I was busy. Perhaps it was just too much effort for a still-grieving mother.

It was late that year when I finally made myself go into the field. I knew winter's cold would soon make walking unpleasant, and I needed to go while I could. I discovered new loops of mowed trail extending out from the center circle. Ribbons and I walked the new trails, but it wasn't the same. The bright flowers were done blooming, and the weeds and grasses were thicker and higher than before. It was not the same beautiful place I remembered.

There is a time for everything, according to Scripture. Perhaps there was a time for the field to be my healing place, and now it is time for something else. The field's delightful new stage of development had coincided with my need for nature's healing influence—but I believe the timing of my "pilgrimage" was no coincidence.

As I had walked the dog in that field, it had become a stage upon which God shared the power and majesty of His Sovereign Being. He showed me a glimpse of Heaven's peace. I felt the magnetic pull of His unconditional love. I realized the joy of having a real relationship with Him—the kind of relationship He desires with each of His children.

I began to understand how healing comes from spending time in God's presence. Though full surrender can be an instant decision, it is also a continuing process as God lovingly reveals layers of resistance that interfere with true fellowship. Gradually, He moves into a deeper intimacy with the human heart and mind—but only as far as we allow His Spirit to enter. Peace comes as we learn a trusting dependence on His guidance and care.

Epilogue

LOOKING BACK

A pilgrimage often changes the pilgrim. Now that I've emerged from my wilderness experience in the Wetlands, have I changed? Am I fully healed of my wounds? Perhaps not. I think I will always carry the scars of loss. Life goes on after losing a loved one, but it is never the same again.

My pilgrimage is past; it's time to refocus on the future. It's time to let go of the sadness and make room for the joy of living to flow back into my spirit. I know in my heart that Bob is safe in his Heavenly mansion, and I will see him again. I still have a purpose here on Earth. As long as I am alive, there is always more to experience and more to learn. Life itself is a pilgrimage adventure, a search for meaning. I will not find all the answers in this lifetime, but I believe the best place to search is in God's word.

What happened in the field and the memory of what I saw and felt is a strong, lasting influence. As I take Ribbons out to the back yard each morning, I glance eastward at the sky over that hidden place. I look for the rosy glow that sometimes touches the clouds for a few brief minutes, and I remember how God's presence touched me in that nearby field. A beautiful morning sunrise still gives me hope and joy. Grateful for the memories of all that God has done, I know it's time to put what I've learned into daily practice.

Through all the painful times that God has allowed in my life, I have seen that He has lovingly taken care of me. He has guided, protected, encouraged, and given comfort—even when I was not aware of it until later. I am thankful for every precious moment that He shared with me in the Wetlands field. I believe He used that place to remind me of the joy of intimate fellowship and to teach me how important it is to nurture that relationship.

For too long, I had told myself I needed to spend more time with God; yet I had put it off. Then one morning I sensed a change in my attitude. I suddenly realized what a precious gift I was avoiding—an intimate love relationship with the Almighty God of the Universe. I could personally tell Him my fears and needs in prayer. I could read His Word—His love letter to mankind—filled with stories of His compassion for His people. I could meditate on the deeper meanings of His Word and its application to my own life. If I took time to wait quietly in His presence, to open my heart and listen; I could sometimes experience God communicating with me. This was a profound privilege, not an inconvenience!

Any change of perspective comes not from one experience only; it is a result of many things. I'm sure my experience in the field was an exceptional influence. God speaks in many ways; to know that the voice I hear is His, I need to stay close to Him. The more I read God's Word and seek to understand who He is, and the more time I spend just being alone with Him, the more I sense the blessing of His presence.

One morning as I looked around at the piles of papers on my office floor, I spoke aloud in frustration: "Where do I start?" Perhaps to avoid the dilemma, I decided to open my inspirational book of "Morning Meditations." And the first words of that day's message were: "Where do you start? You start with Me!" Reading those words left me in awe of God's amazing Sovereignty; I see that He rewards and encourages those who seek Him!

Again, I resolved to take time for regular prayer and Bible reading. One Scripture passage seemed to reveal new truth; another reminded me of something I'd forgotten. Each day inspired me to return for more. My relationship with God was coming alive again—outside of the field.

I wish I could say I haven't neglected that relationship since then, but I get distracted too easily by things I need to do. Even so, God has never stopped working with me, and I haven't stopped trying to do better—again and again.

In spite of my fearful reluctance when life seems scary or overwhelming and in spite of my headstrong ways, He still leads me to places and experiences that reveal new insights. He still reminds me that I need to focus on Him and depend on His resources. I need to trust in His guidance and allow His perfect love to overcome my fear and uncertainty. Sometimes I wonder: will I ever learn? I praise God for His mercy and patience.

I am grateful for the vision of those who worked to restore a piece of farmland into something so priceless to this grieving mother. That field with its cheerful flowers and the peace of nature's influence was the ideal setting for my pilgrimage of healing. It had been there all along within walking distance beyond the edge of our community, just as God's presence is always waiting beyond the edge of our own self-assurance.

God led me to that secluded field for a reason. I call it my healing place, but it was a special "Holy Land" where I found renewed fellowship with His Spirit. He showed me a promise of hope in a glorious sunrise. He gave me a vision of His Sovereign glory and power as I watched the awesome movement of clouds. I rested on a man-made bench by a man-made pond, but I worshipped the God of all creation as the sun gave light to His handiwork. Alone in that open field, I experienced God's love reaching out to me through the beauty and peace of His natural creation.

As my husband once told me, we all need something to look forward to—something to help us through the hard times. God has promised a future in Heaven beyond our comprehension; He has given us something to look forward to that is greater than anything here on Earth. Beyond the visible edge of this life is a glorious eternity.

On one particular day while walking in the field with Ribbons, a simple incident revealed powerful insight to help me deal with my own fears of tomorrow. As Ribbons and I entered the field, I often took her off the leash. Because I could trust her to come when called and not run away, I gave her the freedom to enjoy her own exploration. When it was time to start back, she seemed eager to go home without running ahead. When I stopped at the edge of the field, Ribbons would stop beside me and look up expectantly. "Let's go home, Ribbons," I often said as I snapped the leash back on her collar.

It occurred to me—that it might be just like that when Jesus takes my hand with those same words: "Let's go home, my child." He will carry me away in His loving arms to my own Heavenly mansion, to leave behind all the fear and uncertainty, and the unimportant clutter of this life. Like Bob, I will find myself in a new dimension— in a world of love and light and goodness, surrounded by joy and beauty beyond anything I've ever known. I will have a healthy new body and a life free of sadness and pain. Why would anyone be afraid of that? Why would anyone not look forward to it? Remembering God's words of assurance three days before Bob died has given me hope for my own future.

Fear of death is a natural human viewpoint; we dread the progression and pain of illness and aging. We fear the unknown, and we don't want to leave the people we love. We mourn when a loved one is gone, but that process itself is our healing. Death is the doorway into the Heavenly dimension. Death is the surrender of this imperfect life in order to be with the perfect One who died to provide a perfect future. Because I believe in Jesus, He will give me victory over death. And the older I get, the more I would appreciate a new body!

My own final moments wait somewhere ahead, veiled by God's grace until their appointed time. I don't want to spend the rest of my life worrying about when or how or where; God alone has that knowledge. I must use my time wisely, and I must trust my Heavenly Father to take care of me whatever happens. He is able, in spite of my uncertainty.

I am trying to overcome my worries by remembering my husband's words—to look at this beautiful day God has given us and enjoy life's blessings with a thankful heart. When difficult days come, perhaps God's Spirit will again whisper reassuring words to encourage me. I receive what I need when I need it, and usually not until then. I must be patient. I am sure there are more struggles ahead for me, but I will try to remember each one has a purpose. Since I can't fix every problem the way I want, I need to keep doing the best I can and to trust that God is with me. God says I am never alone.

Perhaps I also need to consider that obedience is based on trust; and as I trust His power, He enables me to be obedient. When doubts and fears begin to overshadow my faith, I know I have lost focus on His Sovereignty. Too often I see only my human weakness; each morning, I need to see the hope of a sunrise and a fresh new vision of God's love and power. I need to remember what Grandpa Moats told me: "God has always taken care of us."

A beautiful mountain scene once hung on my wall. Printed across the bottom was a quote by Ralph Waldo Emerson: "All I have seen teaches me to trust the Creator for all I have not seen." As I learn to know the peace of fully trusting my Creator, I can willingly go forward to unknown places.

Bibliography

Blessing our Goodbyes... a Gentle Guide to Being with the Dying and Preparing for Your Own Death...by Kathie Quinlan. (A practical aid for caregivers, with one chapter on grieving)

Don't Let Death Ruin your Life, *a practical guide to reclaiming happiness after the death of a loved one...*by Jill Brooke

Facing Death and the life after...by Billy Graham

Healing After Loss...Daily Meditations for Working through Grief...by Martha Whitmore Hickman. (A collection of inspirational thoughts)

Jesus Calling... Enjoying Peace in His Presence, Devotions for Every Day of the Year...by Sarah Young. (A devotional that challenges my perspective)

Lament for a Son by Nicholas Wolterstorff. (I love his writing style and format)

Living after Loss…Helping you on your journey through grief… by Sandra Myer. (A Christian mother shares how her faith in God helped her through her own journey of loss)

Morning Meditations from your Abba Father by Alyse Best Muldoon. (My favorite devotional when I long to feel God's presence)

The Wonders of Nature…365 Devotions Celebrating God's Beauty…edited by Barbara Farmer for Worthy Inspired.

In addition…Elisabeth Kubler-Ross and David Kessler have written several books individually and together:
Life Lessons
On Death and Dying
On Grief and Grieving
The Needs of the Dying

Other books by Betsy Kelleher:

***Sometimes a Woman Needs a Horse**—a personal story of discovery of a spiritual message in the horse and rider experience* (Published in 2004 with Pleasant Word/Winepress). The first edition was awarded First Runner-up in the Legacy Nonfiction category of the Eric Hoffer Awards for 2009. A revised second edition was published in 2014 by Xulon Press.

MARES! (Ya Gotta LOVE 'em) – Fifty Stories to Aid and Inspire Mare Owners – Compiled of stories submitted by horse owners across the country, published in 2008 by Xulon Press.

Although both books are no longer available online, more information can be found on her website, www.goduseshorses.com along with many of her columns written for the *Illinois Horse Network* newspaper. For almost twenty years, Betsy's columns appeared under the heading: "Sometimes God Uses Horses," sharing her experiences with horses from a Christian perspective. Readers may contact this author by email at goduseshorses@aol.com.

Printed in the United States
by Baker & Taylor Publisher Services